A BELIEVER'S FAREWELL TO RELIGION

A BELIEVER'S FAREWELL TO RELIGION

ROGER LENAERS, S.J.

CARYSFORT PRESS

A Carysfort Press Book

A Believer's Farewell to Religion
by Roger Lenaers, S.J.

A translation by Dan Farrelly of *Gläubiger Abschied von der Religion*
published by Edition Anderswo, Kleve 2015, which had been translated from
the Dutch *Al is er geen God-in-den-hoge*, Pelckmans, Kapellen, 2009

First published in Ireland in 2017 as a paperback original by
Carysfort Press, 58 Woodfield, Scholarstown Road
Dublin 16, Ireland

ISBN 978-1-909325-47-0

©2017 Copyright remains with the author
Typeset by Carysfort Press
Cover design by eprint limited
Printed and bound by eprint limited
Unit 35
Coolmine Industrial Estate
Dublin 15
Ireland

CONTENTS

PREFACE

A Believer's Farewell to Religion

The very title of this book reveals a relationship in content to a book published by the same author in 2010 called *Living in God without God*. But it is more than a mere relationship: it is a continuation. Through the shock of its paradoxical and consciously provocative title, *Living in God without God* was aimed at communicating the insight that the little word "God", unproblematic though it might seem to be in the way we use it, can in fact, in the context of Christianity, lead us along very different paths – at least since modernity began to flourish with the arrival of the Enlightenment. Earlier, in the pre-modern Christian culture "God" was an unambiguous quantity which gave no rise to misunderstandings. Precisely because the reality to which this little word refers is so eminently important to every believer, it is likewise important for him to be conscious of what he thinks is the content of the word and to what extent, in the modern world, he can still accept this content.

We owe the stimulus for this awareness to Dietrich Bonhoeffer who, in two theologically rich letters written from the Nazi gaol in Spandau 1944, for the first time – and still in a preliminary way – formulated his new insight: "We should live in the world as people who deal with life without God." He no longer had time to pursue his insight in a systematic form: in the spring of 1945 he was hanged by the Nazis in Plötzensee. The provocative title of the first book has its origin in one of those two theological letters, where Bonhoeffer writes, as a summary of the modern Christian's purpose in life: "In God's presence and with God we live without God." Many believers will have problems with such sentences – and this is only one of many in the two letters. But *A Believer's Farewell to Religion*, the continuation of that book, is based without fear on the same fundamental conviction. Thus it seemed necessary, at the beginning of this book, to take up Bonhoeffer's insight again and only then to begin with the continuation of the ideas proposed in the first book.

The title *Living in God without God* laid down the direction the book would take: it would deal with the practice ("living") of a

Christian faith ("in God") which, as with modernity, has integrated departure from *theism* ("without God"). This practice of faith has two aspects: an ethical and a mystical aspect. *Living in God without God* was deliberately limited to the ethical aspects of a belief in God in which modern man can feel at home. Thus the book unfolded a Christian ethics which was a departure from a law-giving, controlling, and rewarding or punishing *theos*, i.e. a pre-modern God-in-Heaven, and was feeling its way as it turned to the incomprehensible sacred depths of reality.

Following Jesus and inspired by him, the modern believer sees and believes these sacred depths to be unconditional, unlimited love. And challenged by the modern theory of evolution he interprets the cosmos and its laws as the continuous self-revelation of this love which, in the course of the cosmic aeons, expresses itself with gradually increasing clarity. On every level of evolutionary history this fundamental reality reveals itself as love, i.e. as the drive towards unity, and this with ever greater intensity, beginning with the atomic level. For atoms are only the result of the growing together of subatomic elements which become fixed to one another with unimaginable force. Precisely the intensity of this binding force gives us an idea of the completely supreme level of the force suggested by the words "Fundamental Love". Then, when the first unit is formed this force moves the atoms to join together into still more complex unities, and molecules are formed. And that is not the last word, not by a long way. The molecules, for their part, are clearly driven to form still greater and more complex unities – proteins – until out of these extremely complex forms a living thing develops, which realizes a much more intensive inner unity than all previous phases. After the beginning of life, for a few billion years a blaze flares up of ever new and more complex and amazing forms of life, in which gradually animal consciousness awakens and the search begins for encounter as in socialization and in the forming of groups and sexual union, until finally in man the level is reached on which it is possible to speak of selfless love. The ethical law is nothing but the experience of this evolutionary drive developing within man, urging him to further growth in love. The appropriate ethics for a modern believer is therefore an ethics based on love.

What this love, both human and divine, concretely demands is seen by the Christian in the actions and thinking of the historical person Jesus of Nazareth. In this way the Christian discovers the course that love wants him to take – in other words, the concrete content of his ethics of love. *Living in God without God* presents this content, characterizing this ethics, showing how it is distinguished from traditional church ethics and in what way it is better.

What has been said here is clearly different from the usual idea of evolution in which evolution and creation appear in competition, even as irreconcilable opposites. It seemed therefore useful, in the first chapter of this book, after the encounter between modern atheism and the Christian faith, to look more closely at the meeting between evolution theory and the belief in creation.

But ethics is only one of the two aspects of living in God without God. There is a second aspect which is just as important which was referred to above by the perhaps misleading name "mystical" and which could also be called "spiritual". "Living in God" does not merely amount to ethical practice. It demands also a consciously lived encounter, a becoming one with the Fundamental Love, God. In other words, it requires prayer. And this, too, has two aspects: personal prayer and prayer in common – connected with ritual, which in the Christian tradition is called liturgy. We are heirs to a Christian past in which both of these aspects of prayer have been richly developed and cultivated. And where believers' inheritance has been influenced by modernity it encounters two great hindrances which stand in the way of the enjoyment of this inheritance. First there is the conception of God that appears everywhere in the wealth of traditional prayers: namely, the pre-modern image of a *theos* outside the cosmos, a God-in-Heaven. And the modern believer feels estranged from this image. Even for his own personal prayers he has great difficulty in falling back on the treasures of tradition. The liturgy is brimfull of formulae and customs and prescriptions, all of which have their origin in a far-off pre-modern past. For modern man this past is gone; it has become an unreal world. For him those words and ideas no longer have any real resonance, and he can no longer honestly deal with them. For this problem, which was not addressed in *Living in God without God*, an answer will be sought in the present book.

But because liturgical prayer and the activity of believers are reduced as a rule to participation in (or presence at) Sunday church services, two critical chapters will deal with this part of the liturgy which has its unassailable central place. Departure from the pre-modern God-in-Heaven has far-reaching consequences for the notion of what happens in the Eucharist. Departure from the *theos* means departure from the sacrificial cult and prayers of petition. The *theos*'s need for bloody and unbloody gifts, the so-called sacrificial gifts, and its sometimes hesitant willingness to hear our prayers (and then mostly after prolonged begging on our part) are so thoroughly anthropomorphic that the modern believer can, of course, no longer take such an image of God seriously.

Church prayers are continually taken from the riches of the Bible, where the church at least unconsciously assumes that it finds there the words of an anthropomorphically conceived divine communication. It should therefore be made clear just how far a modern believer can go along with this. Therefore this book also devotes two chapters to a critical examination of the way in which the church – not just the Roman Catholic Church, but equally the other Christian churches – understands the Bible and explains its content. This discussion will lead to another statement which will elicit loud protests from pre-modern believers of all churches – not only the Roman Catholic Church – that the Bible is human communication. This statement, however, can be supported by quite solid arguments. But this criticism of the Bible is not a denial that its authors were at pains to give verbal expression to the authentic inspiration which they experienced deep within themselves, using the limited and limiting means available to them in the mode of thinking and speaking in their culture and in their own psyches. Therefore, in the context of modernity we can also still speak of "Holy" Scripture. In the Bible texts the breath of divine inspiration which gave rise to them is still present. It is true that this is not always easy to trace because it is overlaid with the strangeness of cultures which are long since extinct. But it is nevertheless still in evidence, since the words move our hearts to goodness because our belonging to the same humanity enables us to recognize as our own the experiences recorded long ago.

In summary: both *Living in God without God* and *A Believer's Farewell to Religion* describe what follows when one attempts to situate the Christian faith in modern culture, which, while it is essentially atheistic, is only such insofar as it denies the existence of a "Big Brother" outside the cosmos of whom there are no traces in our own world. What would be the basis, then, for a reasonable person to affirm such an existence? Moreover, the qualities of this *theos* which believers uncritically affirm are not only purely anthropomorphic. They contradict one another: father and judge, lover and executioner, almighty love which, however, does not step in to protect wretched and suffering humanity from disaster. The idea proposed by Nicholas of Cusa that God's essence is an *identitas oppositorum*, an identity of opposites, also offers no solution here. Perhaps the mysterious and for us incomprehensible aspects of God's being do coincide. But in our concepts, in the thinking on which our communication is based, they are mutually exclusive. The coincidence of opposites is therefore unthinkable and not real. The inevitable solution can only be that we give up the traditional anthropomorphic image of God, despite all the worrying consequences which come with such a step. The aim is to seek the true God of whom the traditional image is only a transitional, inadequate sketch which has been overtaken by evolution.

R.L.

Vorderhornbach

15 December 2016

Chapter One

An Old Affliction: The Conflict between Faith and Knowledge

Science and Christian faith always enjoyed the mutual understanding of a happily married couple in the past, at least until the 18th century. Until then all the great names in science were Christian believers and many of them were even quite pious. We can think of Copernicus, Vesalius, Mercator, Van Helmont, Galileo, Torricelli, Keplcr, Pascal, Descartes, Newton – to name only some of the best-known. Even Darwin in the 19th century was a confessing Anglican Christian, and Mendel was a Benedictine monk. Moreover, even at the time of the *Encyclopédie Française* it was still acceptable in polite society to speak of the "Great Architect of the Universe". In the 17th century the pair did have a couple of brief quarrels, first when Giordano Bruno crossed the boundaries of church teaching with theories which were condemned – but have since been acknowledged as visionary – and which brought him to the stake on the Campo dei Fiori in Rome; and then when Galileo, in the opinion of the same church leadership, endangered the contemporary inviolable worldview by his convictions based on astronomy. But only in the second half of the 18th century did the domestic bliss of the pair begin to go seriously awry. The tensions led, in the 19th century, to separation, and this led to bitter divorce proceedings in which each party attributed the blame to the other.

There is more than one reason why the originally friendly climate which had existed for 1000 years between the two parties changed, in a fairly short time, to enmity. The first and most important reason was the church leadership's fear of the Enlightenment ideas which were quickly spreading in educated circles after 1750 and shattered their world like an earthquake. They had taken fright already in the first half of the 18th century at the deistic notions of the Free Masons and had reached for the cudgel of excommunication, though without much success. Precisely their continuously greater condemnations resulted in the Enlightenment, which was clear about its evidence and conscious of its own value, and turned in understandable anger against the Church. The way the Church reacted proved that it was blind to the truth or, worse still, wanted to be blind and did not want people to enjoy their full rights to take on the full maturity which had been refused them, and to realize a form of society whose banners bore the magical words liberty, equality and fraternity. The Church leadership, too, would be on the side of fraternity as long as it did not threaten the hierarchical superiority. But liberty and equality publicly contradicted the superiority given to them by God and were therefore seen as inspired by evil forces.

Soon, in its anger the Enlightenment not only turned against the Church, for which it had good reason, but also against religion, for which it had less good reason. What was probably the decisive factor in this was that it knew religion only in its ecclesiastical form and identified religion with this form. In the collective consciousness of the West other religions played no role: they had never seen them as having any value but only as dangerous errors, like Judaism and Islam, or as shameful superstitions to be done away with, like the polytheistic cults which had been encountered in America and Africa and had been combatted with zeal for the faith.

The leading minds of the Enlightenment were not statesmen but thinkers. In France, the cradle of the Enlightenment, they were called *les philosophes*. But their philosophical ideas gradually influenced political society and thus laid the foundations for the anti-Church volcanic explosion of the French Revolution. After being absorbed and then developed further in the 19th century by Feuerbach and Karl Marx, the ideas of the Enlightenment led in the 20th century to an aggressive atheism: in the Soviet Union, in Mao's China, and in today's North Korea. This atheistic way of thinking is characteristic also of modern non-Marxist philosophy, for anyone who professes that freedom and autonomy belong to the essence of man cannot at the same time say that man is dependent on a power outside the cosmos. These two are simply mutually exclusive.

A second factor which contributed to the divorce was the sacred alliance in France, which was at that time the think-factory of Europe, between throne and altar. This alliance gave its blessing to social injustice, and this made of the God proclaimed by the church a socially reprehensible, oppressive power. The call for action for the French Revolution became also "*Ni Dieu, ni maître*", neither God nor master. Up to the 18th century people had for the most part borne injustice with patience, in the erroneous conviction that it was the will of God. But in the 19th century it was confronted with the new democratic ideas of the rights of man, equality and freedom and it provoked organized resistance. A God who gave his blessing to injustice had outlived his usefulness. Marx and Engels in particular were the spokesmen of this anti-religious tendency.

Science becomes atheistic

Up to the middle of the 19th century criticism of religion had remained the domain of the philosophers. Feuerbach had prepared the way, and thinkers like Marx and, later, Nietzsche had taken his insights and developed them further. But until then the scientists were quite able to cope with a God who did not disturb them in their work. But now some members of this pious guild began to get the impression that this was no longer the case. The God they had heard about in their catechism classes was supposed to be an omnipotent force up above, always able to intervene at will in the activities of man and in the processes of nature, and did in fact occasionally intervene without worrying about the laws of nature which had painstakingly been brought to light and were held to be unalterable. If only there was somewhere evidence of this omnipotent force! But no, there was nowhere any trace of it and its activity. All that in our ignorance we had earlier attributed to its activity we now saw has intra-mundane causes and can reliably be explained without reference to an interfering God-in-Heaven. Isaac Newton, the brilliant physicist and astronomer, had at the beginning of the 18th century still given the place of honour in his syntheses to God, with deep and uncritical piety. At the end of that century everything had changed. The answer the astronomer Laplace gave to Napoleon to whom he had described his astronomical system and whom Napoleon had asked about the place of God in it – since he no longer appeared to be in it – is well known: "Sire, we no longer need this hypothesis." That was not a profession of atheistic unbelief; it merely showed that it is possible to give a coherent explanation of astronomical phenomena without bringing forces of a non-cosmological kind into play.

But the disappearance of God from scientific discourse meant a noticeable bolstering of atheistic thought, for whereas philosophers develop personal insights which are only of interest to those who are on the same wave length, scientists have the firm ground of facts under their feet. And whereas the normal person in the West knows hardly anything about philosophical thought processes, the media have to a large extent popularized scientific discoveries and thereby made them accessible to people with a normal education. Criticism of religion coming from a scientific angle is bathed in an aura of reliability, which by the same token strengthens its influence.

Just as with the philosophers, the anti-religious crusaders from the ranks of the modern sciences are concerned with the defence of human autonomy, here more specifically in the form of the autonomy of scientific thinking. The idea that a force from outside the cosmos could interfere at will in the processes of nature undermines the brand-new edifice of scientific syntheses. The laws of physics and chemistry lose their power, cease to be laws, and are reduced to statistical probabilities. And to build on this is to build on sand. Biochemical reactions can then run quite differently from what could be expected on the basis of exact calculations (in such cases the Church would speak of miracles), and that would be very annoying. The theories which succeeded in putting the results of research at our disposal would only be partly reliable. That would mean the death-knell for modern science. Anyone who relies on science and makes scientific research his life's work has to be appalled at the idea of a God-in-Heaven who interferes at will.

Moreover, a fundamental principle in the practice of modern science is that every statement must be verifiable, i.e. able to deal with the most stringent criticism. But what is maintained about the other world, which is always poised to intervene, is never verifiable and lacks all reliable foundation. But taking unfounded statements as a starting point has to lead to chaos. Mediaeval medicine, satirized by Molière in *Le médecin malgré lui*, can serve as a model. It was in every respect a product of time-honoured convictions which were in no way based on experiment and research, and the result was quackery that would make one's hair stand on end.

And then came Darwin, and the results of his scientific research, without his wanting it, gave the deathblow to the reliability of the biblical story of creation. Darwinism thus became the root of a long and bitter conflict between modern science and the Church's faith. For traditional Jewish-Christian believers it was absolutely necessary to retain the biblical notions. The Bible was, after all, the word of God. The whole of Christian teaching depended on its reliability, and likewise the whole Christian worldview was based on this teaching, and without it there was no inner security.

This was, especially for the Church leadership, a question of survival. With the downfall of the Bible would come the downfall of their power and their financial security. Up to the beginning of the 20th century Rome also stubbornly maintained that the modern ideas about the stories in the book of Genesis were reprehensible and beyond redemption, that God really did model Eve from one of Adam's ribs and that this couple was immortal until it lost this privilege as a punishment for disobedience. And this teaching had to be instilled into future priests in their theological education. Doubting the historical reliability of the book of Genesis, and naturally even more denying it, was punished by the Church leadership in Rome with the few methods which they still had at their disposal: withdrawal from a teaching post, ban on speaking and writing, sacking, and even excommunication. Really they were trying above all to convince themselves. For if already in the first two chapters the Bible could lay no claim to reliability, how reliable was it in the other chapters? And could it still be called the word of God? Fear of a collapse of the intellectual foundation on which it rested was haunting all the churches to different degrees. Religious resistance to Darwinism came from deep within the human psyche. Where this is the case the most logical arguments and proofs count for nothing. In such cases the heart has reasons which the ratio does not know.

The fact that the battle has not yet been decided becomes clear if we look at the situation in the US, which is, after all, highly developed and modern. Astounding as it may seem to an educated European, half of the US population constantly defends the historical reliability of the biblical creation stories and on this basis rejects the theory of evolution. Despite palaeontology and geology and all the fossil discoveries, they still maintain that God created the earth about 7,000 years ago. You can calculate that with the Bible in your hand. Pressure of modernity has at least achieved one thing: the other half of American citizens have begun to think differently about it. One section of this modern-thinking half accepts Darwin to the extent that they extend the six days of the first creation story to six geological periods so that there is room to account for the fossils which are millions of years old. Of course, that was not what the biblical author had in mind, for he based the Sabbath rest on the seventh day on which God rested, and the Sabbath is definitely a day made up of 24 hours and is not a geological period. The other section of this modern-thinking half is further advanced and has done what is obvious for us: it affirms the theory of evolution. Whoever does this can naturally no longer read the first chapters of the book of Genesis as a reporting of fact. They are seen as a form of profound story-telling with a religious message which tries to give an answer to questions about the origin of the world and humanity and about the "why?" of suffering and death.

Creation and the theory of evolution are irreconcilable enemies?

Along with these there is in the US a swiftly expanding group of scientists who reject not only the biblical creation stories as completely unfounded but also every religious interpretation of the processes of evolution. They are called Neo-Darwinists. They think Darwinism through to its logical conclusions, with more consistency than is found in our devotees of evolution theory. These latter do not see what the Neo-Darwinists do see: namely, that the traditional theology of creation runs counter to an honestly thought-through theory of evolution and even to modern science. Thus it is not possible to believe in a creator as the churches do and at the same time adhere to Darwin's theory of evolution. Yet Christians who follow evolution theory have no such qualms. Clearly they do not (as yet) notice the contra-diction. What follows here is an attempt to show this contradiction and then to overcome it.

What is the content of the traditional teaching about creation? That a force from outside the cosmos calls into being all the processes taking place within the cosmos, continually controls them and also, as it were, from outside guides the coming into being and the further development of living things. But modern science sees no trace of such guiding activity. All processes faithfully follow their own inner laws. They proceed according to intrinsic and exactly calculable chains of cause and effect without any noticeable influence or intervention from outside. Belief in an extra-mundane activity therefore has no basis other than tradition, which falls back ultimately on personal, unverifiable opinions which one has, through dependence and ignorance, accepted as truth and handed on to others. There is no proof for this piously accepted extramundane activity. And this activity also adds nothing to what has already been coherently explained.

In the US, anyone who does not want to discard the traditional teaching about creation has been called "creationist". However, not discarding the teaching about creation does not amount to seeing the notions in the book of Genesis as a factual report. But the refusal of the American creationists to give up the biblical presentation of creation despite the crushing evidence of evolutionary science has brought with it a stuffy sense of backwardness. And that has dire consequences for the three religions which adhere to the book: Judaism, Christianity and Islam, for in each of the three the existence of an almighty creative power is fundamental to their religious teaching. The Christian profession of faith, for example, both in its short form – the twelve articles of faith – and in the longer creed of Nicaea-Constantinople, begins with the sentence: "I believe in God, the creator of heaven and earth", in which the expression "heaven and earth" is a Jewish expression for the more abstract "everything". And the Vatican's *Catechism of the Catholic Church* devotes no less than 100 paragraphs to this confession of faith. According to this, everyone who subscribes to this confession of faith would be a creationist, and therefore every Christian a backward person. That compels us to ask whether faith in a creator God is compatible with modernity and, if so, under exactly what conditions.

In answering this question we should always keep in mind that traditional talk about creation includes, in principle, the creator's freedom to intervene at will and at any time in cosmic events. But there is no longer any room in modern thinking for such interventions. It can therefore be no surprise that more and more scientists, and especially more and more evolutionary biologists, call themselves atheists. Their spokesperson is the brilliant English evolutionary biologist Richard Dawkins. For him, religion is a disaster for today's humanity because it shuts off access to (scientific) truth. His books, translated into many languages, are bestsellers, which points to the fact that they give expression to the as yet unconscious notions and hunches of many modern people. People like Dawkins know that a doctrine of creation filled a need as long as there was no better explanation for the origin of life and of the infinite varieties of species. But that time has passed. The scientifically based doctrine of evolution which we owe to Charles Darwin and his successors has brought it to an end.

Around 1860, with his book *Origin of the species by means of natural selection,* Darwin was the first to provide the indispensable scientific arguments for the evolution and the variety of living things. Specimens which by chance fit in better to their environment have better possibilities of surviving and handing on these advantageous qualities to their offspring. Others in the struggle for survival in competition with their better adapted counterparts have drawn the short straw and gradually die out. On the basis of this survival of the fittest, of those better adapted to their environment, a continual process of natural selection takes place. Evolution and the infinite variety of living things is simply the result of this natural selection.

But where do these better qualities come from? They are by no means the result of inheriting acquired qualities, for there is proof that these cannot be inherited. Shortly after 1900, half a century after Darwin, Hugo de Vries solved the problem. They are the result of spontaneous mutations in the genetic material. Cosmic radiation and chemical influences cause chance minimal changes in the genes. These mutations can make an individual capable of resisting the pressure of his environment. They can also, conversely, lessen his chances of survival. If a mutation is an improvement, the offspring inherit this improvement and hand it on to their own offspring. After some time a small favourable mutation takes place in one of these offspring and its offspring then profit from it, which gives them an advantage over other members of their species. In this way evolution continues, at an infinitely slow tempo. If a mutation is harmful the effects are the opposite. The new combination proves to be defective, sometimes even lethal. If it is lethal the poor creature soon dies, also without progeny. And if it does have progeny these die in competition for survival against the improved members of the species. The whole living cosmos is therefore the result of a mass of chance mutations combined with natural selection over millions of years.

Along with mutations and natural selection an incalculably long period of time is to be seen as an indispensable third factor. Favourable mutations are a rare occurrence. Mutations can be compared with a hunter who only shoots wildly around him. He may happen to shoot a hare but the chances that he will return home with an empty bag or accidentally shoot another hunter are clearly greater. Precisely because the favourable mutations occur so seldom the evolutionary process requires astronomically long periods of time. However, at the end of this boundless stretch of time, that which the amazed observer spontaneously attributes to the genius of a higher intelligence is the result of the described process of undirected mutations and natural selection over the course of an endlessly long period of time. And so there is no direction, no plan, and therefore no creation – for anyone who makes something is looking for an outcome. And then there is no God who creates everything. And so a Neo-Darwinist has no problem with regarding the human eye simply as the end product of millions of flukes.

Interventions from a supernatural world are therefore superfluous; they would even disturb the flow of the processes and spoil things for the scientists. Every honest Neo-Darwinist would have be appalled when advocates of the creation theory maintain that without the mysterious working of an intelligent force outside the cosmos the amazing result of evolution could not be sufficiently explained and that, along with the laws which evolutionary science has brought to light, the intervention of an unverifiable supernatural force is required. Therefore the Neo-Darwinist not only aggressively rejects the crude creationism based on the biblical idea of the six days of creation (and therefore has the creation of the sun coming after the creation of plants, as if photosynthesis were possible without the sun), but also the belief in creation of those who at the same time accept the theory of evolution, as Rome does at present, without being aware of the contradiction between the two simultaneous convictions.

Of course, Neo-Darwinism cannot think it has given a satisfactory answer to all the puzzles raised by evolution. There is still a host of unanswered and perhaps unanswerable questions, like how, through chemical changes in the genes, consciousness can come about, since it is entirely different from the chemical processes in the brain and in the nervous system. Precisely these unanswered questions are the weak point where the opponents of Neo-Darwinism apply the crowbar. Even when they accept all the results of evolutionary biology and thereby put down deep roots in modernity, they still want to leave room for creative activity on the part of God. They attempt this by recourse to the idea of the "intelligent design".

The intelligent design

According to this idea, the whole evolutionary process obeys its own laws and autonomously goes its own way, i.e. without outside interference, yet the end result is much too complex and at the same time too well ordered to be explained by a chance and essentially chaotic play of non-directed mutations. Evolution must be based on a plan deriving from the hypothetical initial big bang. An almighty creative power, precisely by means of this intrinsic plan, would be present at every step of the autonomously flowing process – not by intervening from outside, but by having given a direction and having shown paths in the original plan. In this way the autonomy of the cosmos and the reality of a divine creator would be upheld.

In the 1990s in the US this idea found resonance through the work and publications of the microbiologist Michael Behe and the mathematician William Demsky, and it can reckon on the support of an influential and financially powerful group of American believers who want to clip the wings of atheistic Neo-Darwinism by using the idea of intelligent design. In the meantime, the idea of intelligent design has spilled over to Europe. In the Netherlands, for example, an education minister put forward the plan to expand the teaching of evolution in secondary colleges to include the idea of intelligent design, a venture which met with indignant reactions. In Austria and Germany it was a newspaper article by the Archbishop of Vienna, Cardinal von Schönborn, in *The New York Times*, which inflamed the dispute between proponents and opponents of the theory. For a long time the papers were full of contributions from either side. Both groups were clearly fighting for a cause that was dear to them, which explains the occasional vehemence of their reactions. One group was fighting for the recognition of human autonomy and the other for upholding a religious worldview. And each of the two groups saw the views of the opposing side as extremely dangerous to the good of mankind.

Is it possible to reconcile divine creative activity and autonomous evolution using the idea of intelligent design? And if not, is reconciliation at all possible? A "no" as the answer to the second question would mean that a scientist who is a believer would be condemned to a schizophrenic position. And what is still worse, religion would in this case no longer have any chance in the modern world. For in the modern world science is the iron pot and religion the earthen pot, and when these two collide it is not difficult to predict the result. A very unpleasant prophecy for anyone who considers religion as indispensable for the further humanizing of the world. It will become clear below that the contradiction between the two world views is completely the fault of a pre-modern way of thinking. If we succeed in understanding the relationship between God and the cosmos differently the contradiction will disappear.

In any case, the opponents of atheistic Neo-Darwinism score points when they say that the result of evolution gives the impression, even the overwhelming impression, that it is led by an amazing intelligence. It is incredibly complex and at the same time perfectly ordered, two qualities which are characteristic of intelligent activity. Opponents can highlight a series of "errors" produced by evolution which seem to contradict the idea of intelligent planning, but they are totally insignificant in comparison to the infinite number of cases which give the strong impression that startling brilliance is at work. And that is not to mention the often breath-taking beauty of the result.

Despite this, to write off as a *fata morgana* the impression that there is a plan and therefore an ordering intelligence should at least require that a convincing reason be produced. And nothing in the scientific domain necessarily calls for such a desperate rejection. Science only shows the link between cause and effect and delivers no arguments for or against the activity of a creative intelligence. It does rightly require that no elements be slipped in which are foreign to the scientific investigations, for example, interventions from somewhere on high. And, in the opinion of the Neo-Darwinists, that is precisely the case when one attempts to explain cosmic evolution by linking it with the concept of creation. Their rejection reveals the honest concern that the affirmation of the overwhelming impression of intelligence and recalls the abdicated extramundane watchmaker and thereby torpedoes the autonomy of man and of the cosmos. Understandably they rise up in opposition to this, for belief in autonomy is the foundation of modernity and of the reliability of the sciences, and accordingly of the blessings which these have brought with them. They are happy to leave out of the discussion the negative aspects of these so-called blessings.

But anyone who has found his way to a modern, inner-worldly faith sees the basic error in this thinking. It derives from the short-sighted view that every conception of God inevitably makes of the cosmos an enormous Punch and Judy show. But that is precisely what the modern believer's view of God does not do. If the reconciliation between science and Christian faith is ever going to be achieved it is here. Not in the theory of the "intelligent design", since this theory unconsciously goes back to a God outside the cosmos, and evolutionary biologists like Dawkins are very aware of this. Reconciliation only comes about when we speak and think about God in such a way that human and cosmic autonomy are not jostling one another but that each is completely acknowledged in its own right. For perhaps then it will even be possible to provide a deeper foundation for autonomy than modernity can give and to supply an explanation for some problems in evolution which have not yet been solved – like the emergence of consciousness. Precisely this can be achieved by modern inner-worldly faith.

Creation as self-expression of the absolute transcendent spirit

In the parlance of the modern believer the little word "God" no longer refers to a being outside and above the cosmos but to a transcendent spiritual reality, which is beyond all things and which, as the evolving cosmos, reveals itself and is still completely superior to this cosmos. The following presentation is not aimed at proving the absolute necessity of interpreting the cosmos in this way but that one is equally justified in interpreting it in this way and that one can therefore believe in a creative fundamental reality and, at the same time, in the autonomy of the created world. A comparison may be helpful here.

Let us take a Mozart piano sonata. It consists of delightfully cascading sounds, and therefore of air vibrations. These affect our eardrums and from there are converted, via wondrous paths from the inner ear to the cochlear nerve, into electrical impulses which stimulate the brain and thereby produce audible sounds. In this whole process there is nothing which cannot be purely scientifically observed, although it remains a mystery, even for Neo-Darwinism, how material stimuli can at the same time be conscious phenomena. No matter what, the sonata is much more than a sequence of air vibrations with varying wavelengths which can all be accurately measured and described. It is the conversion of something which is of an entirely different order – namely Mozart's inspiration – into material waves. It is the embodied spirit of Mozart, his inner self, which manifests itself in this material form. This spirit is not an added-on something which a very exact analysis of the sound waves could bring to light. However, no one would consider it sheer nonsense and scientifically unsustainable to speak here of inspiration, and therefore of "spirit", nor would one consider that acknowledging the reality of this spirit might be a threat to the scientific explanation of the phenomenon of music. This spirit does not interfere from outside with the elements that constitute music. It adds nothing and takes nothing away, and yet it is precisely that which brings the whole sound phenomenon into being and permeates it. It is the reason for the existence of the whole and is the ultimate explanation of its beauty. The miracle of sound is the spirit itself, expressing itself in matter. And precisely this is what we call creation. What the artist does is nothing but express his inner self in the stubborn material – which is obviously suitable to be permeated by spirit. In his creative activity man reveals, brings out, ex-presses what lives within him and would otherwise be inaccessible for all, including himself, and would remain hidden forever.

Mechanistic Neo-Darwinism interprets the cosmic miracle as the product of the interplay of undirected mutations and natural selection in the course of immeasurably long periods of time. But nothing prevents us from seeing in it the self-revelation of a fundamental spiritual reality which, in the evolution of living things (and even before the emergence of living things), makes something of his inner self visible which would otherwise remain inaccessible for us. Understood in this way, there can be no problem with interpreting the cosmos as creation. Creating is no longer the making of something out of nothing, to which an impoverished church doctrine has reduced it; it is self-expression in matter, and creation is the gradual self-revelation of a mind that transcends all things.

This interpretation sheds light on something which remains unexplained in the mechanistic hypothesis: namely, that consciousness can emerge from the unconscious. The concept spirit is a name for phenomena which have to do with conscious-ness and which lead to a much deeper level than the material and the mechanical. But to speak of a creative spirit is to speak of a spiritual and therefore conscious fundamental reality. Then it is not at all strange that the self-expression of this spiritual reality should, in the course of evolution, take on first the form of animal consciousness and then the form of the human spirit. These forms were already imbedded in matter from the time of the big bang as if in a congealed state from which they develop and become, as it were, like fluid in the course of the cosmic ages. This is why Teilhard de Chardin does not speak of dead matter but of matter which is not yet living. In matter there is an impulse towards life and consciousness, and in this impulse the active presence of the already-named spiritual fundamental reality reveals itself as it strives to express itself ever more clearly. Mozart taken to infinity, and at the same time purified of the inadequacies which comparisons always entail.

The concept creation also needs to be purified. Talk about creation belongs to comparative language and here lurks the danger that we unconsciously understand the relationship between God and cosmos as comparable with, for example, the relationship between the sculptor and the sculpture. But these stand opposite one another, remain outside of one another, and belong to two distinct worlds. Then the creator becomes a being outside the cosmos, and we fall back into the pre-modern way of thinking. We are protected from this by the conception of creation and the continuous, progressive self-revelation of a transcendent spirit in cosmic form. Or, as a mystic from Islam says: creation is the invisible which has become visible as world.

The path followed by this self-revelation is the same as in the hypothesis of chance in Neo-Darwinism, namely, an un-interrupted sequence of undirected, ever new mutations which improve one another in the course of astronomically long periods of time. But this path is not disadvantageous to the creation character of events. Creation does not mean adding and intervening from outside. It is self-expression from within and is determined by the laws which operate within the cosmos. This is no different in all human creative activity, which is under-standable, since precisely this activity is the model used in the believer's interpretation of cosmic evolution as creation.

This new way of seeing creation has surprising consequences. First, that it is more deeply religious than the traditional view. The mystery, God, feels like a reality that is much closer to us. We encounter him in all that is, since everything is part of his self-revelation. He no longer lives in his own second world. He is still deeper in me than my own deepest self: *intimior intimo meo*, as Augustine of Hippo said in this famous formulation. But this all means that the cosmos and all that it contains is "holy" and is therefore to be treated with reverence. Precisely the holy character of the world makes it a sacred duty for every believer to protect nature, to fight for the preservation of the rain forests, for the multiplicity of species, to fight against extravagant waste, pollution and the devastation of our wonderful blue planet, even more than caring for our health, our prosperity and the chances in life of our progeny.

Second, that this fundamental mystery, God, is striving to become man. Here we are encountering an early Christian concept, but one which has a meaning quite different from the traditional one, in which the "Son" of God in a very late point in cosmic history – namely, about 13 billion years after the big bang – came down from heaven and took on "flesh" that as yet he did not have. No, God's becoming man means, in the modern sense, that the progressive self-expression of God, i.e. the evolving cosmos, has advanced with infinite slowness to hominization, to the emergence of *homo sapiens*. Only this view of things explains something which atheistic humanism also believes without being able to explain or prove it, namely that man has an absolute value and inalienable rights. In the humanistic view this *homo sapiens* is (only) a member of the great family of mammals, no single member of which has absolute value and inalienable rights. So, whence does man derive this value and these rights? He has them because, for the time being, he is the highest form of self-expression of the absolute. And while we protect as sacred the whole cosmos and all that lives in it, we must protect mankind much more.

Third, that fundamental reality expresses itself also in cosmic laws. And because these laws steer all natural processes they are the deepest foundation of every process in nature. But the deepest foundation of a process cannot, as it were, intervene in the process from outside. Thus everything that is attributed to a divine intervention, such as revelations, commands, hearing of prayers, miracles, punishments, becomes inconceivable. It is absolutely necessary that the traditional teaching which sees these interventions not only as conceivable but as quite normal ("for God nothing is impossible") be re-thought and newly formulated.

The advantage of such a view by comparison with a materialistic Neo-Darwinism is evident. What is first seen as an evolutionary process without direction and therefore without meaning becomes here a joyous and wonderful whole. Man is now a searcher after meaning; meaninglessness robs him of his joy in living and of his inclination to act. But for the followers of Neo-Darwinism the whole evolutionary process is completely devoid of meaning. The best they can do is to acknowledge with amazement the staggering perfection and beauty of the results of this directionless and meaningless development. Their attitude cannot be seen as completely logical, for on the one hand they know that successful products of human origin always suggest the work of an ordering intelligence and, on the other hand, they insist that the much more successful products of natural evolution have come about without an ordering intelligence. Just how intelligent and successful these products are is seen from the fact that human intelligence often copies them in order to improve the results of its own ingenuity. Added to this is the fact that the inner-worldly believer's view is extremely optimistic. If evolution has already crossed the threshold of hominization, it intends to proceed further and will. Therefore humanity has a future even if we are not able to describe it in detail.

The single great difficulty for a believer's view of this kind and which does not trouble the Neo-Darwinists – although it is a problem for the creationists – is the problem of evil and of suffering. How is it that out of a fundamental reality which Christians, following Jesus, proclaim to be perfect love, disaster can come – such as earthquakes, tsunamis, drought or floods – causing thousands of deaths? There is no satisfactory answer to this distressing question. We can only try to lessen, to some extent, the severity of the problem. For example, we can ponder that earthquakes and tsunamis are only doing in a few minutes something which is going to come about later anyway: the suffering and death of human beings, the decline of cultures, the destruction of all human achievement. But such an answer is only postponing the problem by dividing it up into a hundred thousand individual problems, each of which is much smaller yet big enough that all of them put together have a shattering effect. And yet it is also true that cosmic evolution without death is inconceivable. Every level of development achieved has to be surpassed and left behind, not simply wiped out but, in another form, taken up into something new; and taking on a new form means giving up the old one and dying. Even stars die.

But the ethically evil, like the holocaust and the gulags and the endless spilling of blood in the course of history – how can it be part of the self-expression of a fundamental reality which is love and perfection? For these horrors are surely obvious forms of refusing to love. At least that is what they look like. Self-expression of love cannot be the opposite of this? It is our belief as Christians that the essence of ultimate reality is love, and here we rely on the message and the life of Jesus of Nazareth. For Teilhard de Chardin, all of that evil is an unavoidable stage in the increasing self-revelation of love, unavoidable because of the inherent imperfection of every transitional stage of the perfect. Another tentative answer might be: with my reason I cannot put together in my mind good and evil, i.e. love and its denial. In logic they are mutually exclusive. To grasp this paradox conceptually is beyond the limits of my mind. In the preface we mentioned Nicholas of Cusa's idea that God's essence is an *identitas oppositorum*, an identity of opposites. Even if Nicholas is right it is no help, for in our conceptual thinking good and evil are mutually exclusive. And what I am unable to conceive of I am not able to affirm. But I must choose. This is an unavoidable necessity. Either I must confess to love being the foundation of all things despite the fact of evil not being in harmony with it, or I must say that everything is devoid of meaning despite the overwhelming impression that the cosmos and life are rich and meaningful. Personally, I choose the former. I dare to make the leap, despite everything, I trust in love. Despite the thousand voices screaming at me about the contradiction between my choice and the reality of suffering and evil. The inner peace and fulfilment which I experience in this choice are my guarantee that I have chosen correctly. Like someone who at night in pitch-darkness is following a path. He does not see the path but with every step his feet feel that he is on the right track.

Chapter Two

Encounter with God in Atheistic Modernity

It is clear that the transition from a pre-modern to a modern image of God must have profound consequences for doctrine, for ethics and for prayer. It has the clearest consequences for doctrine, since the modern view of God is characterized by the refusal to divide reality any longer into two worlds: the divine and the human. The name God now refers to the deepest foundation of all reality, including my own reality. This deepest reality is therefore, as formulated by Augustine, *intimior intimo meo* – more myself than I am myself. God is therefore never outside of the cosmos. But it follows that the possibility of a descent from the divine region into ours disappears. There are no longer two domains, so that, to the dismay of pre-modern believers the incarnation of God drops out of the creed. Then Jesus, too, in contradiction to the council of Nicaea and all subsequent councils and to the whole of church tradition, is not true God from true God. But this creed is the keystone of the whole arch of Christian doctrine! How can this arch survive? Amazing as it may seem, it can, as the book *The Dream of King Nebuchadnezzar*, which can only be mentioned here, shows in detail.

But leaving behind the traditional image of God must have considerable consequences for ethics, for it means parting company with the Bible's anthropomorphic image of the divine law-giver who, like earthly rulers, decrees laws and prohibitions and metes out just punishment to those who neglect his commands. But if the figure of the heavenly ruler disappears the laws and prohibitions disappear with him. The pre-modern law-based ethics which depends on him then collapses. And because ethics is the foundation of human culture it would be catastrophic for humanity if this traditional ethic were not to be replaced by another. In fact a new ethic does emerge from the new image of God. It is just as much influenced by belief in God and in Jesus as Saviour as in the pre-modern Christian ethic and has no less a humanizing influence. What this ethic looks like can be seen in detail in the already-mentioned book *Living in God without God* [Carysfort Press, 2017].

A changed image of God must also have far-reaching consequences for prayer. Praying means becoming aware of transcendental reality, aligning oneself with it, relating to it. In all religions this relationship had always been the highest priority. And it is understandable why. Growth, weather, health, fertility, security, peace – most of these do not rest in our own hands. And yet survival depended on them. But an invisible power (or powers) was clearly involved in cosmic events. If one could move these powers to intervene a big step towards security would be made. But in what way, with what means could man persuade them to act to his advantage? In the same way as he moved the inner-worldly powers on whom he was dependent. He should therefore humbly beg them, and speculating on their greed (for he thought that they, too, shared this with the powerful on earth), bring them gifts, the so-called sacrifices. The connection to the gods thereby took two forms: petition and sacrifice. Relinquishing the pre-modern image of the rich ruler on high with whom we could achieve something through petitions and sacrifices and recourse to mediators and patrons must mean that prayer has to be of a different kind. This is the subject of the present chapter.

Spirituality as the leading edge of prayer

Praying means, as we have said, making a conscious connection with transcendent ultimate reality with which, by existing, we are always unconsciously connected. Existence is sharing in the fundamental reality that encompasses all things. Conceiving of this reality as an anthropomorphic *theos* (or as a multiplicity of such *theoi*) or – as in a modern view of God – as Fundamental Love manifesting itself in the shape of the cosmos, is a secondary consideration. The central concern is the conscious link with this reality. But under this, as a continual support, is a *subconscious* attitude out of which the conscious link can blossom at any time: it is called spirituality. In accordance with the disposition of the subjects and with historical influences this basic attitude can take on many colours and shapes, so that we can speak of spiritualities in the plural. But as a general concept spirituality refers to a constant attitude that looks below the surface of reality, does not reduce it to what is pleasant and useful, or unpleasant and harmful, but in the spirit of the letter to the Philippians (4:8) "is concerned with what is noble, pure, kind, virtuous and praiseworthy". This attitude can exist without conscious religious orientation. Spirituality can, in other words, be a-religious, god-less. And because it is something constant, permeating the whole of existence and enriching the deeper level of the person's existence this attitude is more important than religious orientation and its conscious manifestation as prayer, just as the essential is more important than the specific and the constant more important than the transitory.

The spirituality of a modern believer has much in common with the pre-modern – even the essential and most important things: both are equally an affirmative (though implicit) answer to the self-revelation offered to us by God, however one thinks of him, whether in a pre-modern or in a modern way. The reason is that in contrast to the case of prayer, in spirituality the differing views about God hardly play a role at all. Here the essential point is its attention to the deeper level of everyday reality. In this respect it is completely secondary whether one is a modern or pre-modern believer. As such, both pre-modern and modern spirituality belong equally to the "penultimate". What counts is the purity and intensity with which one looks for the "ultimate". In bike-riding it is not important whether one has at one's disposal 18 gears or only three but how strongly one pedals. Nevertheless, there is a modest advantage in having 18 gears.

What is the modest advantage enjoyed by the modern believer's spirituality? First, that it makes clear what the concern for everything which is noble, pure, kind, etc., which Paul encouraged the Philippians to foster, has to do with the "ultimate". For it makes clear that everything, of itself, has to do with this. The depth of reality, the level therefore with which all spirituality is concerned, is in the modern believer's view just another name for Fundamental Love, which is God. In the pre-modern view, on the other hand, a connecting link is needed between our inner-worldly and therefore meagre virtuous activity and the holy mystery which is God. The link is the task imposed by God-in-Heaven to do good. Only the decision to carry out this duty links human activity with the divine world and gives it "eternal value". That explains the pious custom of offering to God, in advance, the day and all that it will contain, as if what we do and omit to do had, on its own, nothing to do with God and were of no lasting value.

Modern spirituality has yet another advantage. Pre-modern formulated faith has made of the loving fundamental reality an anthropomorphic *theos*, a ruler modelled on man. But this model tends to reflect human failings and errors as well – like pride, arbitrariness, bias, hypersensitivity, extreme severity, even mercilessness and corruption. Such an image of God will necessarily influence and put a strain on prayer, which is the conscious encounter of a God represented in this way. But it will also harm spirituality: in everyday life one will allow oneself things which are a contradiction to genuinely Christian spirituality, with the justification that this is the way God himself acts or in this case would act. This explains, for example, that St Bernard of Clairvaux, full of fire, could summon men to the second crusade with the words "God wills it" (did God really want it?), or that pious members of religious orders acted as judges in the witch trials or in the dreadful tortures carried out by the "Holy" Inquisition.

Many Christians have to a large extent corrected these shady sides to their lives because they have let themselves be moved and led deep down by the humanity of God. Think of the endless procession of saints in the still pre-modern church and, above all, think of Jesus, who like his whole Jewish community was pre-modern in his thinking and found his inspiration in the pre-modern Bible and yet experienced no disadvantage in it. But most Christians, and even the saints in their own way, have suffered from the pre-modern image of God in their fear of laws and the punishments connected with them; or were intolerant, since also the *theos* was seen to be intolerant; or by manifesting neurotic traits or practising self-torment – of a kind that is incomprehensible today – as a consequence of applying inner-worldly legal norms (guilt demands penance!) to their image of God which had in it much of the all-too-human judge.

But we should not lose sight of the plus points of pre-modern spirituality. A first plus point was that God, in their view, required prayer and demanded it so definitely that praying and religious exercises often characterized the whole of life. What developed from this was a very rich prayer culture which has handed down to us immeasurable treasures in forms of prayer. Unfortunately, the heavy stress on the need and importance of prayer brought with it the danger that piety took over the entire horizon of man's relationship with God, often to the detriment of action that was pleasing to God. The figures (or caricatures) of the Pharisees in Luke 18:10-11 and in Matthew 23 illustrate this danger.

A second plus point of pre-modern spirituality is that it has produced a powerful religious culture. This may indeed be full of the image of the anthropomorphically conceived *theos*. But it provided protection against the reduction of human life to a materialism which had no horizon but knew only the categories advantageous (or harmful), and pleasant (or unpleasant). Pre-modern religious culture achieved this through buildings and images – the towns of the Middle Ages were full of churches and pious statues and paintings –, through customs like ringing bells, muezzin calls to prayer, processions, religious feast-days and pilgrimages, or through precepts and prohibitions, like laws regarding eating, and Sabbath prescriptions. These all kept the link with the transcendent alive and explain that even the 250 precepts and the 365 prohibitions of the Torah were not an unbearable burden for the Jews; many of them were glad because every precept and prohibition could mean an encounter with Yahweh in everyday life. The breakthrough of modernity and the disappearance of the second world make it impossible to think this way any longer. This means that products of the culture of that time no longer awaken any religious consciousness, no longer point to the divine. Cathedrals, with their religious art treasures, are now only visited because of these treasures. They have become museums. This impoverishment has the meagre, positive advantage that the shady reverse side of this religious culture, the lack of humanity, also belongs to the past.

Prayer in pre-modern piety

Out of the soil of spirituality grows prayer. This connection has as a direct consequence that without spirituality, without a lasting awareness of the essential – the deep dimension of everyday reality – true prayer will never come about. At best there will be petitions, cries for help when the situation becomes unbearable. But then, when one finds help from somewhere or other or the danger disappears of itself, the cries for help immediately stop. Praying, by contrast, is a personal encounter which is independent of chance emergency situations.

We are heirs to a Christian past in which prayer has undergone rich development and been cultivated. But when the heir is a believer influenced by modernity there is a great hindrance to his assuming this inheritance. The image of God which pops up everywhere in the rich prayer tradition is the pre-modern image of a *theos* from outside the cosmos, a God-in-Heaven. And the modern believer cannot warm to this image.

Pre-modern piety can be characterized by the concept cult. This concept, which is derived from the Latin word *cultus*, includes recognition of a person's own insignificance and of the superiority of the revered *theos*, and through his name underlines the gap between the two. He knows that one does not speak to a ruler on the same level. Acknowledgement of the superiority of the *theos* was expressed in those days in a variety of ways, for example by the size and luxury of the cult buildings and altars, through rituals incorporating veneration – like genuflections, prostrations, songs of praise, incense, valuable gifts presented to the *theos* and in some cases destroyed in his honour. And through petitions.

For petition is also a form of this recognition. Primitive man in need of help experienced more clearly than we do that he was threatened and powerless and dependent on those invisible beings which manifested their terrifying power in natural phenomena. In his precarious position what could he do? Only beg for the mercy and help of these powers. Petition is historically the basic form of prayer. It is clearly the older of the two brothers, petition and praising. As long as the relationship between man and the gods was only one of need and lived dependence, petition was appropriate and the climate was not yet ready for encounter and therefore for prayer. It is said that need teaches us to pray. The reality is that need only teaches us petition aimed at the removal of need. Once need is gone, petition is gone with it. Hopefully gratitude is then awakened and with it true prayer.

Petition may well have been the original form of praying, but in the light of a modern conception of God it is by no means its fundamental form. Prayer is, as we have said above, the conscious link with "God". But in the modern believer's view "God" no longer refers to a *theos* that is prepared to give help and gifts or is to be pacified, but to a creative love driving the cosmos on to further development and man to further humanization. In what form will the encounter with Fundamental Love, i.e. prayer, be realized for the modern believer?

Obviously in the form of surrender. For what is the first thing expected of us by the love which moves us? That we let ourselves be moved by it. This surrender has both an active and a passive side. The active side consists in our taking care not to cling on to anything. We should let ourselves be led by that infinite creative movement, obey its thrust, and no longer yield to our inclination to determine everything ourselves. We should, as well, listen to the voices of our intuition and our reason (for it is through these that the impulse of love expresses itself in our consciousness) and do what these voices tell us. The French Jewess and mystic, Simone Weil, calls this attitude: "*se laisser faire*", literally, to be accepting. In everyday things, she says, we always have the choice between doing and not doing; in our relationship to God we only have the choice between letting things happen to us and not letting things happen.

The other side of surrender, the passive side, consists in willing acceptance of what we cannot change, no matter how bad it is, in the certainty that Fundamental Love is revealing itself also in this form and even here is still Fundamental Love and speaks personally to us. And that we can do no better than surrender to it, to let ourselves be taken over by it. In a short poem of Erich Fried which enumerates the things we would prefer to escape from, the refrain is: "It is what it is, says love". The first half of this line, "It is what it is", sounds fatalistic. It admits that one cannot change the reality no matter how much one would like to. But seen as a whole the refrain is anything but fatalistic. It presents love as speaking to us, and love calls on us to affirm reality, because love itself is the reality, which is thereby good, painful as it may be on this occasion. For it has concern for us and, despite everything, wants what is good for us. Hence the hint of fatalism disappears. On the basis of such an attitude, Alfred Delp, arrested by the Nazis and seriously maltreated in prison, was able to write from his cell: "The world is full of God. It comes to meet us, streaming out of every pore of things." Out of every pore of things, not just out of the pleasant and enjoyable ones. But we do not willingly let ourselves be taken over, we continually defend our little self in us (here man is confronted with the mystery of the evil that lives in him) and thereby remain alienated from the deepest foundation of ourselves and from what is our true good. But God does not accept that and wants, despite everything, to fill us with himself. Therefore he never ceases to draw us to himself and he awakens in us through this attraction the need to find him and to become one with him.

This longing is transformed into a petition, but not like most of the pre-modern petitions for something concrete, useful, for help, for the solution of our problems, for rescue from need, for good weather or whatever else there might be. The mystery we turn to and in which we breathe and live is no magician who could intervene in the operation of the laws of nature to fit in with our wishes and in reality disturb the function of the laws. Modern faith only asks for one thing: identification with the Fundamental Love, the end of our alienation from our true good, and ultimately the realization of what Fundamental Love seeks.

Even begging for forgiveness has no meaning in this context. Such petitions only bring into play the slighted master whose anger we want to escape from. But the Fundamental Love, poured out in streams, is never hurt and does not bear a grudge. Only human beings are like that. Does a petition for mercy therefore have no meaning? Certainly it has meaning! For mercy and compassion are different from forgiveness. The compassionate Samaritan does not forgive. He helps a fellow man in need. God's compassion has nothing to do with the "forgiveness of sins". The petition "Have mercy on me/us" is a confession of our profound need which can only be assuaged by the encounter with the eternal beauty we long for.

In contrast to petitions for forgiveness, praising and thanking as forms of prayer can be taken for granted and should never be left out, for we breathe and live in that eternally giving reality. And acts of adoration should also not be missing. They should not be expressions of submissiveness but superlative forms of admiration, astonishment, of lapsing into complete silence. The pre-modern believer takes as his model the Orante, the figure standing in prayer, looking upwards with hands raised to heaven. For the modern believer the model praying person is instead the fish in the ocean. The ocean encompasses him, carries him, keeps him safe, permeates him, nourishes him, gives him breath, gives him life, is infinitely close to him, always and everywhere, and praying seeks to become aware of this intimate closeness and to surrender to it.

Liturgy as the prayer of the community of believers

The foregoing dealt with personal prayer. This personal prayer is an indispensable condition of liturgical prayer, for without personal prayer the liturgy will never be more than an empty ceremony even though externally it may be of high quality. And it should go beyond that level, for it is essentially the community of believers' encounter with God. And if this is the case, the changed conception of God must lead to a changed form of encounter with God.

Every religion expresses its relationship to God or to the gods in its own way. The liturgy is the Church's form of veneration organized by the religious leadership or by the believers' collective. Like every other cult form, ours too – the liturgy – exists before us. It is free of improvisation by individuals, whereas the individual can freely improvise his own personal prayer. The individual has to slot into the liturgy and follow, and in a certain sense submit to, ceremony. Only in this way does he profit from what the community profoundly experiences. This ceremonial form is consciously or unconsciously inspired by the form which in those days (and also today to some extent) one had carefully to observe when one was permitted to appear before a prince or other dignitary. God-in-Heaven, before whom one appears in pre-modern liturgy, is the infinitely enlarged figure of the inner-worldly prince. Therefore there are very precise stipulations as to what one must say or do according to the circumstances of this holy audience, what clothes are to be worn, with what formulae, gestures, posture the divine prince is to be met, and on what occasions and on what days one is to appear before him, etc. And who prescribes this sacred ceremony in the conviction that he is sufficiently versed in the heavenly ceremony, of which the earthly one is to serve as a model? It is an authority in Rome which feels it has a mandate for this from God-in-Heaven, and with almost scrupulous exactness prescribes what may and may not be done in liturgical celebrations. In this almost fearful concern we find something of the awestricken trembling before the God enthroned in heaven in Isaiah's vision of his being called by God, Isaiah 6. This is paired with the opinion that this sublime God insists that he be honoured by means of such ceremony. This concern also explains the regularly repeated admonitions and warnings from the Vatican or from the bishops that nothing is to be changed in the official texts which have been monitored by Rome and given its blessing. For they are thrice holy. Just how far this Roman authority pushes it is seen from the following extract from the Vatican liturgical decree from the year 2001 about the translation of Latin liturgical texts: "Translating liturgical texts is not a matter of creativity but of fidelity and accuracy in reproducing the Latin original in the language of the country. Expressions like *caro*, flesh, are to be translated literally and not by abstractions such as self-seeking. Verbs are to be translated very precisely with regard to person, number and form (active or passive). Provision of new texts can only be authorized by the Bishops' Conferences. These new texts must exactly reflect the style, the structure, the choice of words and other traditional features of the Roman rite." But in a modern view of faith the traditional notion of a God-in-Heaven – of a prince surrounded by a heavenly state court – has had its day. This means that most of these prescriptions regarding ceremony are bereft of meaning. Despite all Vatican admonitions they are therefore no longer binding.

However, ceremony is not meaningless in itself. It is based on the idea that the external should not contradict the internal. The external is the expression of the internal. The ceremonial prescriptions mirror externally the way we experience reality inwardly – or should experience it; and to this extent it is meaningful and therefore also binding. At funerals there is no dancing or waltzes or uncontrolled jumping about. Not because it would be forbidden but because such exterior behaviour is not in keeping with what the company experiences in these moments. Through clothing, posture and gesture we show one another what we are inwardly experiencing. Therefore, the leader of the liturgy is not going to stand before the congregation in frayed jeans and a sleeveless T-shirt but will wear clothing appropriate to the occasion, basically according to a ceremonial form. One can pray in one's pyjamas in private, but not at the altar. Everyone senses this. But the reason is not that I can also not appear in pyjamas before a head of state, because that would mean that here again we would be degrading God to being a projection of human rulers. That this is not the reason can be shown by the fact that I can pray to God personally in my pyjamas even though I am then encountering the same divine reality. Where it is a question of a collective encounter with the divine depths, the signals I give should not contradict the experience of the collective. Clothing required by ceremonial form breaks through and transcends the superficial level of the everyday. But one could ask whether the whole episcopal and papal wardrobe is really necessary for this, or even the Mass vestments, which even as recently as 1950 were considered so holy and important that the moral theology textbooks considered it a mortal sin to celebrate Mass without a stole, not to mention a chasuble.

A critical look at the liturgical texts

Liturgy is comprised of texts to be spoken and rituals to be carried out. Both are in serious crisis because of the transition from the pre-modern to the modern conception of God. Above all, the texts. These speak the language of the pre-modern past and are therefore full of the notion of God as a mighty, even *almighty* king up above. Hence the stress on distance to God and the important role of prayers of petition, confessions of guilt and begging for forgiveness (rulers are very sensitive in things that regard themselves). Intercession also has an important role to play. This comes from the idea that, just as with human rulers, nothing can be achieved without the intercession of advocates at God's lofty throne. Because of the pre-modern notion of God there is also a proliferation of concepts which no longer have any resonance with modern man: such as sin, guilt, punishment, expiation, penance, or out-of-date theological constructs which are supposed to be articles of faith, like the sacrifice of the cross and Mass as a sacrifice. Such language, despite its dignity and literary perfection, no longer promotes the modern believer's encounter with God. It does not correspond to its notions about faith and cannot express them. It is little more than a lofty jingling of words. For the modern believer it makes no sense to go along with it.

And so what should he do? Stay away from the liturgy? But that would mean staying away from the Sunday Mass, since for nearly all the faithful the liturgy is to all intents and purposes limited to this. And the celebrations of Sunday Mass are the indispensable gatherings of the community of believers. That is where the Church becomes visible. It is where it comes about. And we need these meetings with our co-believers for the strengthening and confirmation of our faith and theirs. This is precisely what the words mean, that the living Jesus is creatively in the midst of his disciples. And so we should not stay away but patiently put up with what we cannot change. As a last resort we should install an internal transformer in order to convert into modern believer's terms the valuable things that come to us in mediaeval packaging.

With luck one might find a group in which the liturgy is more in line with the sensibilities of the modern believer and in which, despite all of Rome's directives and prohibitions, texts are used which correspond to the modern believer's ideas. The liturgical texts are essentially meant to be the bread which nourishes the community of believers. But in many cases this bread is so old that it has become as hard as stone. And we should not forget that the traditional texts did not fall down to us from heaven. They were made in those days by people like ourselves – by people of that time, for people of that time – as an expression of their encounter with God at that time. If it was good to do that then, surely it cannot be bad to do the same now?

For modern believers the liturgical texts should reflect a different view of God from that of a heavenly king, of a state court surrounded by angels and saints to which we may turn only in accordance with approved ceremonial forms. Therefore we need liturgical texts which express our encounter with the fundamental miracle, which is God, in such a way that the community of modern believers can identify with it. It is certain that we cannot expect such texts to originate from Rome. And also not from the bishops, who are always squinting in the direction of Rome. Therefore we have to create them ourselves, as Oosterhuis has done in the Dutch-speaking area. But that presupposes in the person who ventures to take it on some insight into the faith and some experience of prayer. And creativity and literary talent. Every director of the liturgy should really be able to make prayers freely as he speaks. Protestant directors of liturgy prove themselves on average to be superior to Catholics in this respect. That is not at all surprising, since the Catholic clergy simply lack this tradition. It was never allowed to do otherwise – and has never done otherwise – than read off the texts in the Missal as prescribed by Rome.

But without the support of personal prayer – and this applies to the faithful as much as to the liturgical directors – the liturgy is at best an aesthetic experience, and in the normal case a collective exercise of duty, where the best moment is the "Go in peace".

Rituals

However, liturgy is not just a collection of texts to be spoken. It is also a totality made up of rituals to be performed: rituals help us to cross the boundary between matter and spirit, to escape for a moment from the sphere of the useful, and therefore of the objective, and to enter a deeper level: that of the essentially human. Animals have no need of rituals. They live completely on the level of the useful and the pleasant. Human beings need rituals precisely because they are essentially not useful. That is what characterizes them. They are not a means to achieve anything else. This is precisely what makes them precious. When, with their help, we leave the sphere of the useful, i.e. of the surface, the deeper level of the transcendent, of the truly fulfilling opens up. In this way they are experienced as an enrichment and are gladly repeated. This is true also of profane rituals like knocking, and standing up when an important visitor arrives, shaking hands or embracing when we meet people, or standing up straight when a hearse is passing by. It applies even more with regard to religious rituals, such as joining one's hands or kneeling down or lighting candles. These make the as yet nameless encounter with the transcendent to some extent into a conscious encounter. And then there are the rituals proper to Christianity, like the blessing of fire and water, the song of praise for the Easter Candle, the signing with ashes, the veneration of the Cross, the procession of the Blessed Sacrament, and church burial. These give the religious rituals an expressly Christian colour. They recall that in Jesus transcendent reality is approaching us.

From the multiplicity of Catholic rituals the seven sacraments stand out. For the higher value attributed to them by comparison with the other rituals tradition calls on the idea that in the performance of the ritual God-in-Heaven himself intervenes (and here again ceremony plays a role) by, for example, taking away original sin, by infusion of grace, remission of sins, exempting from punishment, turning bread into the body of Jesus Christ, etc. In a modern believer's faith there is, of course, nothing left of these divine interventions. This means that for modern believers the sacraments lose the extra value uncritically attributed to them by the pre-modern faithful who were under the illusion that in these God himself was involved, while all other rituals and prayers were only the products of human beings.

Originally only two rituals were considered to be especially important: baptism and the Eucharist. And they owe their value to their expressive power, as the origin of baptism shows. Being submerged in the water of the Jordan by the charismatic preacher John could be experienced by his listeners as a real rebirth, as the beginning of an existence that is well-pleasing to God. The early church took over this ritual as a sign of renewal which one experiences through faith in Jesus. But signs not only express something, they also confirm that which is expressed. They are creative, exactly as the wedding vows of the couple not only express their bond with one another, but also confirm and strengthen it. Gradually the rituals which seemed to be especially important increased in number until it reached the magic number 7, but at the same time their value as signs decreased. In reality the seven sacraments are hardly signs any longer, although precisely that, in the pre-modern teaching of the Church, is part of the essence of sacrament. They have hardly any expressive force now and they are no longer creative. The only creative activity of the sacraments should happen in the other world, which unfortunately is no longer seen to exist. The sacraments themselves are only signals sent to another world to have it activate its promised intervention. For what expressive power is there in the handful of water which flows over a baby's head in baptism? Can it still communicate the experience of a bathing which causes a rebirth? Or can the touch of ointment on the forehead of a sick person or a confirmand communicate the experience of healing or strengthening? But because they are no longer expressive, because they no longer speak to us spontaneously these rituals no longer have an existential effect. By "existential" is meant precisely that which concerns and influences human existence – concretely experienced life – and is therefore itself able to be experienced. In the pre-modern view the sacrament did not need to have any perceptible effect. Its effect belongs to the other world and is no more noticeable than that other world itself. If the sacraments are valuable, then only according to the measure of their expressiveness, which is identical with the measure of their effect. But since they have been reduced to signals they have lost all expressiveness. A signal does not need to express anything. It only needs to start the agreed activity.

In a modern view of faith the sacraments are not all that important. Their value is primarily of a sociological kind. They give the Roman Catholic Church its particular profile. Without its own profile an association threatens to crumble away. For then it is no longer sufficiently distinguishable from other associations and is no longer held together by this demarcation. This applies also to the Church. Fortunately, the Church as an association is not first and foremost a sociological entity. It is a community which has gathered around Jesus of Nazareth and which lives from an existential bond with him. But this bond is continually activated through prayer. Prayer is therefore more important and more necessary than those seven rituals which only very occasionally activate this bond, some even only once in a life-time. And those that do it frequently easily become reduced to a purely formal act. In any case, more important than the sacraments and more important even than prayer, and even the *only* truly important thing is the way one lives as a Christian: whether and to what extent we let ourselves be led by the spirit of Jesus.

There is no doubt that rituals and signs are good and that some of them are in fact helpful. As a union of spirit and matter we need them, but as modern believers we only need those which do not presuppose a supernatural origin and a supernatural effect. Everything should have an inner-worldly meaning and attraction. If rituals and signs do not help and renew us they have no value even if they belong to the holy seven and the pre-modern Church praises and prizes them and even considers them to be indispensable. The essential, the ultimate, the intimacy with Fundamental Love which is the basis of our existence – all is just as accessible without the sacraments as it is with them. Both are a path to mysticism, if by this term we mean the experience of the unfathomable spiritual depths.

In a pre-modern view, with the consciousness or objectification of this experience a kind of separation or gap appears. Even without all intimacy with him being thereby threatened or belittled, God remains a reality "outside" or "opposite", as can be seen in the liturgy. In the modern believer's view, however, despite all objectification (without which it is not possible to speak about the experience) one remains no less unified with the Fundamental Love, which is both a person relating to us and is at the same time the deepest essence of our own being. That can earn the modern view of faith the unwarranted reproach of pantheism. Fundamentally we are concerned with the eternal tension between transcendence and immanence.

This has not been an exhaustive description of the distinction between modern and pre-modern spirituality, but it has dealt with a large part of it. And the result is that in a modern-thinking world by far the greater part of pre-modern Christian spirituality is doomed to extinction. That applies to the liturgy directed and controlled by Rome; it applies to the sacraments; to the prayers of petition (insofar as they presuppose a graciously listening God-in-Heaven who then intervenes for the petitioner); to the intercession of the saints to support the petition to a scarcely accessible God high up on his throne; to sacrifice, which is a purely pre-modern and even pre-Christian practice – used mostly as an intensification of the prayer of petition – and is fundamentally a form of corruption. It applies also to self-punishment and self-torture which is given the euphemistic misleading name of penance. In modern spirituality there is no longer room for any of that.

A spirituality which unites

Then what is left of Christianity? The essentials. What Christianity was in the beginning. For then it was not yet a religion but the belief of a community in Jesus of Nazareth as Saviour and belief in the loving mystery with which he was filled and which he addressed as "Father". It has become clear, in the meantime, in what sense this spirituality of the modern believer can be called a-theistic. In its praise it can be said that it can cross all religious boundaries to unite all who in a similar way believe in an inner-worldly transcendence – Buddhists or Yogis or Sufis or Taoists. All of them share the same experience of God as we do. For there is only one experience of God, just as there is only one Fundamental Love which communicates itself. But because of their different cultural backgrounds each group necessarily expresses its experience in a different way. However, the difference in expression is no basis for doubting the authenticity of an experience which is formulated differently, let alone for rejecting it. It is always one and the same Fundamental Love which communicates itself. But each can only give an authentic account of it in the context of its own culture. This makes syncretism suspect from the very start.

In contrast to this unifying spirituality of the modern believer, the pre-modern kind always tended to divide. Think of the intolerance amongst Christians of the early centuries which led to wars of religion; or the punishment with death required by Sharia law if a Muslim converts to another religion (concretely: Christianity); or the laws concerning blasphemy; or the dispute in the contemporary Christian camp about sharing the Eucharist. The difference in the conceptual understanding of what happens in the Eucharist (Is the bread changed? Is it an un-bloody sacrifice? Does the shared creed have the same content, so that we are not deceiving one another? etc.) was enough for a shared Eucharist to be forbidden at the Church Congresses in Munich and for those who ignored the prohibition to be severely punished. The cause is always the theistic illusion that one is in sole possession of the absolute truth because God-in-Heaven is supposed to have communicated it solely to one's own group.

By contrast, the unifying tendency of the modern believer's spirituality corresponds to the thrust of Fundamental Love which in the course of cosmic history reveals itself as striving for an ever richer unity. Just how much this should be part of every Christian's faith can be seen from Paul's intuition where he sums up the meaning of creation, of the church, of Christian life, in the sentence: "so that God may be all in all" (1 Corinthians 15:28).

Chapter 3

But Why Always the Bible?

There is a certain irritation expressed in the title of this chapter. It comes from the circles of modern unbelief. The believer can feel the same irritation if he is surprised on a peaceful Saturday morning by a visit from two Jehovah's Witnesses who want to convert him to the true faith with quotations from the Bible. The modern unbeliever also experiences this irritation when he hears how the Bible is spoken about in church. He can value the Bible as a unique document of cultural history which is referred to in the *Guinness Book of Records* as being indisputably the book with the greatest number of editions and the largest number of translations. Besides, this book has been undoubtedly fundamental to Western culture and has thereby played a decisive role in shaping the modern world. Without the Bible it is not possible to understand this culture. But the Bible owes this important role essentially to the earlier conviction of believers that it contains the word of the living God himself and is therefore sacred and inviolable, a repository of divine truth, a guide to human behaviour, an answer to all the important questions about life.

This conviction, according to modernity, is based on an illusion. Modernity has seen the illusory character of a supernatural world from which the words of these books are supposed to have rained down. Therefore the veneration with which the Bible is surrounded and the bustling activity devoted to it cause the modern unbeliever great annoyance. In his eyes this veneration is of the same kind as the veneration of the Koran by the Muslims. This, too, is seen as the written record of Allah's very own words and is therefore sacrosanct and inviolable, and woe to anyone who desecrates this holy book. To what practices of contempt for humanity this conception leads can be seen from the command to flog or to stone an adulteress. This cruel punishment is then the express wish of Allah, and it is also the express wish of Yahweh in the Bible. And human protests against this divine decision carry not the slightest weight.

Naturally the Church leadership and modern believers are in agreement that the divine authorship of the words in the Koran is an illusion and that the author is therefore Mohammed and not Allah and the angel Gabriel. But just as naturally they totally disagree when it comes to the divine authority of the words of the Bible. The divine character and therefore the absolute reliability and importance of these words are for the Church leadership beyond all doubt. They are consistent in labouring to imbue the faithful with this insight. At least now. The same zeal which they formerly put into recommending non-biblical forms of piety – such as the rosary, devotion to the Sacred Heart, May devotions, 24-hour prayer, atonement crusades, devotion to the saints, processions, pilgrimages, Stations of the Cross – is now put into participation in Bible circles and Bible conversations, attending lectures on the Bible, reading introductions to the Bible. The interest consequently aroused explains the success of sales of the ever new Bible translations and the multiplicity of Bibles for children and young people, pocket Bibles, illustrated Bibles, Bible magazines, books about the Bible, etc.

To make the faithful more familiar with the word of God Rome prescribes that in the Sunday liturgy there should be not only two but three readings from the Bible (which happens hardly anywhere), and forbids replacing the prescribed readings with non-biblical readings (which nevertheless does sometimes happen). And the wording of these readings is considered so sacred that the authorized Roman office forbids any changes being made to the prescribed Bible translation even with regard to extracts where the meaning is not clear even to exegetes.

This is not the only way that the Church leadership shows its conviction that every sentence in the Bible represents God's very own words and that all human interference is taboo. It does the same thing by reinforcing the authority of its teaching through implicit or explicit reference to the words of Scripture. Normally an author uses a reference to indicate that he is not alone in his conviction, that others also think the same – and indeed people of some weight and authority – and that what he writes is not nonsense. But in Church documents a quotation from the Bible generally serves as a decisive argument proving the validity of what the document says. The divine authority of the Bible serves as a guarantee.

Hidden contradictions

But if the Church leadership is really so convinced that the Bible is the word of the living God (this is what the reader at Mass is to announce after the reading) it is very strange that for more than a thousand years it had no problem with seriously hindering access to this word. It did this first by having this word praised as being highly nourishing, to be read out in liturgical gatherings for centuries in a language which only very few of the listeners understood. It did not seem to matter that these listeners had nothing to take home with them from the message they heard proclaimed. The authorities were obviously convinced that hearing the words even without understanding them had a healing and saving function. This corresponded to their opinion that the sacraments which were received without consciousness, as in the anointing of a person in a coma and dying, or in the baptism of a new-born baby, could have their saving effect without fail.

Furthermore, such strong emphasis on the importance of personal engagement with the Bible does not square with the impossibility for believers, over a period of more than a thousand years, of becoming familiar with this word of God except through the liturgy. First, one had to belong to the minority of those who could read at all as well as to the still smaller minority of those who could read Latin. Besides, the Bible was a rare object. In every case it had to be copied by hand – work which required patience – and only monks had the necessary time. Furthermore, only monks in the monastery libraries had access to such handwritten precious objects for the purpose of copying them. That changed with the invention of book-printing in the 15th century. This made it possible for everyone who understood Latin – and had enough money to cover the not inconsiderable cost of buying a printed copy – to read the Bible at home. And since the 16th century it was no longer even necessary to be able to read Latin, for at that time the Bible translations were appearing on the market. From then on anyone who had learnt to read could read the Bible in a language which he understood. Unfortunately, this translation work was done by Martin Luther and other Reformers, which in the eyes of Roman authorities seemed very dangerous to the faith of readers and even a form of betrayal of this sacred word of God. In relation to the

Reformation translation work they paid homage to the saying *traduttore traditore*: a translator is a traitor, a counterfeiter.

But by prohibiting these Reformation translations and allowing non-Reformation translations only under strict conditions they unintentionally gave the impression that the Bible was a dangerous book which was better left alone. Naturally they wanted to prevent the faithful from being infected by heretical ideas. But the actual result of their caution was in contradiction to their claim that contact with the "word of the living God" was of inestimable value. In this way the Bible has remained for the average Roman Catholic a book with seven seals. In contrast to his reformed fellow Christians he has not become acquainted with the world of thought and the manner of speaking of the biblical authors; he has no notion about the areas, the places and persons of which the text speaks and is not even familiar with the names of the books which make up the Bible; he knows nothing of the history and cultural background of what is written; and therefore most of what is in the Bible has no meaning for him. It plays no part in his daily life. He is also not interested in it. The readings from the Scripture at Mass have nothing that he is looking for. In most cases they are merely an obligatory part of the Sunday liturgy and have not the slightest effect on his thinking and living. When Jehovah's Witnesses come knocking on his door, Bible in hand, he feels he has no chance, he is lost, and he closes the door on them in an unfriendly and scarcely Christian way.

Even with a Bible translation and with the aid of a Bible commentary the personal reading of the Bible now recommended by the Church leadership is a tricky undertaking. A normal Bible edition has about 2700 columns, each of which corresponds to a well-filled A4 page. Who has the courage to read through all of this with devotion, or at least attentively? No one reads more than a modest excerpt from the whole. Full books of the Bible are never looked at. Thus one can say that no one reads *the* Bible, not even the keenest advocate of personal Bible reading. At the most, people read things *in* the Bible. And with much of what one reads, and even more with the large amount one does *not* read, one must honestly ask what is supposed to be so enlightening and wholesome in it.

And yet it is said about this book with its myths, stories, ethical guidelines, teachings, sayings, prophecies, that the omniscient and almighty world on which we are so dependent speaks to us, that the Bible is the "word of God" addressed to us. It therefore seems necessary to examine this notion more closely.

The Bible as the word of God

What exactly is meant by the traditional Church teaching that the Bible is the word of God? The Second Vatican Council gives us the following formulation: "These books are written under the inspiration of the Holy Spirit and have God as their author." Everything that the Bible contains, therefore, is written by human authors with God's inspiration. Here the Council distanced itself at the same time from the doctrine which had been taught previously that God had inspired the authors, Hebrew and Greek, in the writing of each single word. With this change of course it solved the problem of verbal inspiration for the translations. Already in the 3rd century in the Western church a Latin translation, the so-called Vulgate, had to all intents and purposes become the Bible. But the words of this Vulgate were Latin words and therefore no longer the inspired Hebrew and Greek ones. Were they, too, words inspired in the translators by the Holy Spirit? At that time it had been necessary to see the Vulgate as also inspired in each word. Otherwise in the Latin West an authentic word of God would never have been heard. But from the 16th century onwards there was a sudden increase in translations into the languages of the many countries, and one could not be sure that every word that flowed from the translator's pen was inspired in him by the Holy Spirit. The Council's solution consisted in not seeing every original Hebrew and Greek word as inspired and therefore free of error but only what is said, i.e. the sentences. Islam, on the other hand, remains true to its idea of word-for-word inspiration of the Koran. Translations are not considered to have the same value as the Arabic original. Therefore in the mosques the Koran has to be read out in Arabic even when no one present understands Arabic.

Divine inspiration really means that the human communications from the biblical authors are at the same time communications from God. How does tradition try to make this unity of divine and human activity understandable? With the help of a dogmatic doctrine which gives rise to as many problems as with inspiration itself, namely, through the Incarnation. Just as according to the Council of Chalcedon (450) the divine and the human nature of Jesus are one "without being mixed or separated", in the same way Holy Scripture is both God's word and human word at the same time. The Second Vatican Council speaks in this context of an "inseparable fitting together of divine and human activity" but does not say exactly in what way the two fit together. Resourceful theologians have tried to explain it with the help of images. The human author can be compared to a musical instrument which is played by God's fingers, or to a secretary who accurately records divine dictation, or to a messenger who delivers God's message. But, as the French saying puts it succinctly: *Comparaison n'est pas raison*: comparisons are not explanations, and theology has since rejected all these attempted explanations as inadequate.

Equating the book written by a human being with a collection of God's own words does not merely suffer from this need for explanation. It suffers at least as much from the many errors in the Bible. Thus not only has the Council given up the idea of word-by-word inspiration but it has also admitted (a quite new view in tradition) that the Bible can contain errors, but only unimportant ones which really have nothing to do with the holy message. But can God make mistakes, even in small things? This, too, would need to be explained. Yet despite all the problems, the churches – the Reformed, the Orthodox, and our Roman Catholic Church – remain unswerving in their identification of the words of the Bible with God's words.

Critical commentary on this identification

The first criticism on the part of modern believers concerns the clear anthropomorphism contained in the identification. We are indeed able to say that God expresses himself, makes himself known, reveals himself in the development of the cosmos. That is meaningful, although it too is a human mode of expression and is therefore to some extent anthropomorphic. But to say that God speaks is a much greater step on the way to anthropomorphism. Speaking restricts human self-expression – which is such a general concept that it can to some extent be used for God – to the production of words, which are sound structures filled with meaning; and to produce these we need lungs, air pipes, vocal chords, mouth and tongue. Only these human sound structures can be recorded with the help of written signs. The Bible would then be such an approximate recording of divine sound structures, i.e. of God's words. The anthropomorphism of this conception goes beyond all bounds.

Secondly, as many a biblical text tells us, the word of God is creative. Therefore, if the Bible is the word of God contact with this word must produce in the hearer or reader a change for the good. But we have said above that the Church leadership thought for centuries that this can happen even when the listener did not understand the text. In this they appealed to what happens in the sacraments. Even though the baby has not the slightest idea of what is happening in the baptism ritual, the baptism would purify it, free it from the claws of Satan and give it eternal salvation. But salvation must be able to be experienced in some way! It is on a deeper level the equivalent of physical well-being, and this too can be experienced. Contact with Holy Scripture must have the effect that one is better off, and that means that one makes progress in being good. And surely one should be able to some extent to notice that! Just as we cater for looking after health, we have to make room for beneficial contact with the Bible. But there is little sign of that. The average church-goer shows hardly any interest in Bible circles, conversations about the Bible, and Bible education. And we can also look in vain for other forms of spiritual well-being as a fruit of Bible readings in Sunday church services.

A third criticism, now in the form of a question, is: how does the Church *know* that the Bible is the word of God? To appeal to tradition only shifts the problem, for how does tradition know? Besides, the Muslims make the same claim for the Koran and the Mormons for the Book of Mormon. Naturally the church rejects these claims as completely worthless. On what basis? In the first instance, naturally, on the basis of its own claim. But that is then only one word against another and not a proven truth against a proven error. But does it have objective reasons for rejecting the claims of its opponents?

Yes, it says. With regard to the Book of Mormon it can use the complete unlikelihood of the story of Joseph Smith. He is supposed to have found, following directions from the angel Moroni, a buried golden scroll which contained the Book of

Mormon. This book was written in a secret language. But the angel initiated him into the secrets of this language so that he was able to translate the scroll into English. When the translation was finished the scroll disappeared as mysteriously as it had appeared. For a sober mind this is a bit much. But anyone who thinks in such a pre-modern way as the Church leadership does must surely accept that for God nothing is impossible? Then why should this extravagant story not also be true?

With regard to the Koran the Church says that Mohammed cannot produce the slightest proof to support his statement that he heard everything word for word from the angel Gabriel. Furthermore large passages of the Koran are clearly copied from the Bible; besides, Mohammed was warlike and practised polygamy, which made his close relationship to God very dubious. But was not Moses also warlike, as for instance his war of extermination of the Midianites in the Book of Numbers 31 proves? And was that other pillar of the Old Testament, King David, not more bellicose than and just as polygamous as Mohammed? And was not the third pillar, Solomon – the model of biblical wisdom – super polygamous with his 700 wives and 300 concubines (cf. 1 Kings 11:3)? Yet these three are seen as reliable mouthpieces of divine revelation.

Instead of highlighting the vulnerability of other revelations the Church should justify its own claim that the Bible is the expression of divine messages – not a book of human words but of genuine words of God. But can it do this? Is it at all possible to know with certainty that the human words are at the same time, and even principally, words of the eternal God? One can confidently think so, because other people whom we consider reliable say it. But they could only say it if God himself had given them assurance about it. And where is he supposed to have given this assurance? Where else if not in the Bible or in the Koran? But this makes one guilty of a perfect vicious circle for offering as proof that which was to be proven. And so there is no certainty regarding the divine origin of the Bible's words, but at the very most surmise and hope.

But surely certainty about this is extremely important. To base one's life on the words of human beings, even on the words of a book considered holy – like the Torah, the Book of Mormon, the Koran or even the New Testament – is a risky undertaking and leads straight to sad excesses, like the extermination of the Inca or Maya culture by the Christian *conquistadores* because they looked on them as heathen and repugnant to God, or like the attack on the Twin Towers on 11 September 2001. Such excesses not only result in a radical rejection of the divine origin of the so-called sacred books but also in an aggressive rejection of every word that claims to come from above. Nevertheless the church unwaveringly equates the Bible with the word of God even though there is no proof at all of this and there cannot be.

The modern-thinking person, also the modern-thinking believer, must reject this identification and as a consequence also the notion of inspiration which it presupposes – and indeed *a priori*. It is based, namely, on the division of reality into the supernatural world of a speaking God and the natural world of listening human beings. And that is a clear denial of cosmic and human autonomy and therefore of modernity. But modernity also argues *a posteriori*. If God himself speaks in the Bible it can contain no errors and can prescribe no unethical laws for life. Otherwise the omniscient God would be mistaken and the supreme judge would be prescribing wrong behaviour. But there is no doubt that the Bible contains a host of smaller or greater errors and often approves of ethically wrong behaviour. Since the New Testament is based on the Old Testament, this will first be proved for the Old Testament.

Erroneous and unethical elements in the Old Testament

The errors in the Old Testament can take the form of impossibilities, contradictions or mistakes. The impossibilities include, for example, the creation of the plant world in Genesis 1,11 before the creation of the sun; or the height of the flood in Genesis 7,20 15 cubits above the highest mountains; or Israel's 40-year period of living in the desert (according to Exodus 12:37 there were 600,000 together with women and children, probably a total of two to three million) where there was nothing to eat and drink; or that Moses was the author of the five books of Moses, although in Deuteronomy 34 he relates his own death and his own burial; or that the sun, on Josue's command (Josue 10:13) stood still at its zenith for 24 hours. Amongst the errors are the mention of camels in the time of the Patriarchs, i.e. c.

1800 BC, whereas these animals were only domesticated around 1200 BC; or that hares are ruminants (Leviticus 11:6); or that Abraham in Genesis 21:32 had dealings with Abimelech, the king of the Philistines, whereas the Philistines only appeared in Palestine c. 1200 BC. The contradictions include, for example, that Aaron in Numbers 33:38 dies on Mount Hor but in Deuteronomy 10:6 in Mosera; or that king Jehu in 2 Kings 10:30 is rewarded for (treacherously!) killing the progeny of King Ahab and then in Osee 1:4 is punished for it.

These are all minor errors, which the Second Vatican Council still considers acceptable because it does not affect the essence of the message. But this is no longer the case where God permits or even demands acts which are inhuman or unjust. We have already mentioned the extermination of the Midianites on the orders of Yahweh in Numbers 31, a genocide in comparison with which Srebrenica pales into insignificance. But there is much more like this. In the Book of Josue 10 and 11, after the conquest of Canaan every living thing in the conquered cities was to be slaughtered. And in 1 Samuel 15:1-3 Yahweh commands vengeance to be taken on Amalec for something which is supposed to have happened 150 years earlier: "Kill without mercy men and women, children and sucklings, cattle, sheep, camels and asses." In the Old Testament, to wage war, always with the help of or in the service of Yahweh, is the most natural thing in the world. Despite its justification of the occasional use of violence, the Koran is, on the whole, much more peaceable than the narrative books of the Torah.

One can hardly speak of justice when, on the express order of Yahweh, gathering wood on the Sabbath is, in Numbers 15:32, punished with death – and, indeed, in a barbaric way: namely, by stoning. Yahweh prescribes the same barbaric punishment for a host of other "crimes": for example, homosexual activity, or fortune telling, or adultery, or insulting one's parents. It is upsetting, too, that Yahweh in 2 Samuel 24 first has King David carry out a census and then punishes him for doing it by having thousands of the people, innocent of course, die. Nevertheless, tradition continues to call the whole of the Torah – hence all of these stories – the word of God, and praises the reading of it as if it brought us closer to God. It is true that only the breakthrough of modernity has opened people's eyes to the ethical reprehensibility of certain acts and customs which were then considered normal, like slavery, genocide, stoning, and the death penalty for homosexuality. But does that mean that in those days Yahweh had an underdeveloped ethical sense?

A final argument against seeing the Bible as the "word of the living God" is an *argumentum ad hominem*. On the one hand the church authorities, out of uncritical fidelity to tradition, accept this identification in its entirety and, on the other hand, contradict it by ignoring, in practice, many important commands and prohibitions of the Torah. They are no longer concerned with circumcision, Sabbath rest, purification prescriptions, dietary laws, the whole sacrificial cult which takes up ten whole chapters in the Book of Leviticus. How is this justified if all of this is the word of God?

The Torah is in reality a Jewish epic

The narrative books of the Torah were earlier always accepted as history. It is true that they contain historically interesting material. But in reality they are not so much history as epic. The content of the Pentateuch, i.e. the first five books attributed to Moses: Genesis, Exodus, Leviticus, Numbers, and Deuteronomy, is hardly more historical than the content of the *Iliad*, and that applies also to the books of Josue, Judges, the two Books of Samuel and the first eleven chapters of the first Book of Kings. Probably Abraham, Moses, David and Solomon did really exist, but what is related about them is a reflection of oral tradition in which the epic condensing and the "joy in story-telling" played a very important role, just as they did in every epic in antiquity.

That the whole has little to do with reliable writing of history was confirmed by recent excavations in Palestine. The narrative books of the Old Testament are clearly the creation of one or several authors from the middle of the 7th century BC who have worked on material of every kind handed down to them, such as songs, myths, sagas, legends, old customs, rituals, chronicles, laws, prayers – and created an epic whole. Whereas in Egypt and in Mesopotamia writing was long since common practice in more developed circles, it appears to have been used in Israel only from around 900 BC, i.e. after the reign of Solomon. Only then did the kings of Samaria and Jerusalem begin, using their scribes, to correspond with the regal courts of neighbouring peoples. Beginning with 1 Kings 12 the content can thereby refer back to kings' chronicles and other written sources, so that the narration becomes more or less historically reliable.

For the dating of the writing down of the Torah around the middle of the 7th century BC the decisive argument is a text in the first book of Kings. After the death of Solomon, under his son Roboam his kingdom fell apart, split into two pieces. Ten tribes formed the northern kingdom and only two formed the much smaller and poorer southern kingdom, the kingdom of Juda with Jerusalem as its capital. In 1 Kings 13:1-2, shortly after 900 BC a prophet from Juda threatened the king of the northern kingdom with a judgement of God because he and his people were besmirching the land with their cult of idols. At the same time he proclaimed on God's behalf that in the far-distant future an ideal ruler named Josias would arise in Juda, destroy the cult of idols in the whole territory of the 12 tribes of Israel, and unite Israel and make it into a mighty state again, as it had been in the time of David. This mention of Josias, who ruled in Jerusalem from 639 to 609 BC is the decisive argument for putting the date of the Torah in the 7th century. The following comparison will make this clear. Suppose a manuscript full of criticism of the selling of indulgences were to be found, seemingly from the 13th century, prophesying that one day a German monk would come and put an end to the sale of indulgences and to simony in Rome. No one would doubt that this manuscript did not originate from the 13th century but was a product of the 16th century.

With their epic creation the authors from the 7th century BC clearly intended two things. The first was religious. The struggle in Israel between the worship of Yahweh and the cult of the fertility gods like Baal and Astarte was still not settled. In keeping with the spirit of the prophets and of King Hesekiah, who half a century earlier had supported the cult of Yahweh, the monotheistic authors wanted to contribute to the victory of the Yahweh cult.

Characteristic of these authors' historical way of looking at things is the way they interpret Israel's political experiences. In their eyes these are not the result of conflicts between the contemporary great powers of Egypt and Assyria and later Babylon which encircled the northern kingdom of Samaria and the southern kingdom of Juda. All that mattered for them was whether Israel had remained faithful to the laws of Yahweh or not. The statement recurs like a refrain that things went well for Israel as long as it honoured Yahweh and observed his laws and prescriptions, and things went badly as soon it ran after the gods of its neighbours. This interpretation is more than just open to challenge, but it is true that precisely fidelity to the law of Yahweh had guaranteed the survival of the Jewish people. The effect was that the Jews thought and lived differently from their neighbours and were thereby separated from them. They were protected from being irredeemably lost in the cultural melting pot of the peoples of the Near East.

The second thing the authors intended was of a nationalist kind. After the decline of the northern kingdom and the destruction of their capital city Samaria by the Assyrians in 722 BC, only the small thinly populated Juda with its insignificant capital city Jerusalem had remained. But if Israel as a whole was really the chosen people of Yahweh it should again become as powerful and rich as in the days of David and Solomon. That was their message. But the power of David and the riches of Solomon were idealized dreams of the 7th century authors, as is clear from archaeological research.

This unity of religious and nationalistic tendencies was meant to achieve two things at once. First, that Juda faithfully followed the laws of Moses so that Yahweh would hold his protective hand over them; and second, that there would be increased readiness to put in the necessary military efforts to re-unify the twelve tribes – in reality these had never been a political union – under the sceptre of Juda. This idealizing writing of history made of the distant descendant of David, King Josias, a messianic figure. He would be the saviour who would make the people of Israel great again. The Torah epic which came about in this way was received with enthusiasm in Juda. It became the spiritual fundamental law of Israel and the foundation of Jewish identity, just as the *Iliad* was to become for the Greeks. This made it inviolable and sacred and it was gradually seen as the verbal record of the promises of Yahweh.

This messianic myth suffered its first blow when King Josiah 609 BC came into conflict with Pharao Necho and lost his life, and a second and much more serious blow when ten years later King Nebuchadnezzar conquered Jerusalem and deported most of the inhabitants to Babylon. A third and final blow was the complete devastation of the city ten years later as a punishment for rebellion. During the Babylonian exile two main elements of the Jewish myth were re-awakened: on the one hand, the need for turning back to Yahweh, for the catastrophe was not attributed to political but to religious factors, namely that Juda had been unfaithful to Yahweh; and, on the other hand, the nationalistic theme: Yahweh would not leave Israel in the lurch and would give his people, north and south kingdoms together, a new future. Especially the prophet Ezekiel promoted this conviction. We only need to read his famous vision of the dry bones (Ezekiel 37) which prophesies that the whole people of Israel will rise again.

Some of this also happened. In the year 539 King Cyrus of Persia had conquered the Babylonians and captured the capital city Babylon. Just a year later he allowed the deported Jews to return to Jerusalem. It is true that after 60 years of exile in Babylon none of the deported had ever seen Jerusalem. Nevertheless, some of them used this permission. Naturally it was those who had been most influenced by the myth of Jerusalem as the city of God and as the cradle of the chosen people. Now in Jerusalem everything was centred around the very modest new temple and the High Priest. The Torah, under the supervision of Esra was revised for the last time. Later the legend would come about, written down in the apocryphal 4th Book of Esra, that the Scripture scrolls kept in the temple had been burnt in the destruction of Jerusalem in 587, but that Esra had dictated them under divine inspiration, and therefore without error, to 40 scribes in 40 days.

The narrative sections of the Bible are "unhistorical"

That the narrative sections of the Bible are unhistorical is more than just probable. What is told about Abraham, Isaac and Jacob in the book of Genesis is supposed to have taken place in the period around 1800 BC and was only written down after a 1000 years of oral tradition. To what extent can such stories be historically reliable? The Vatican has also acknowledged in the meantime that the first eleven chapters of the Book of Genesis is epic writing of a mythical kind. But that means that there is nothing left of the Garden of Eden and the fall of man. There is also therefore nothing left of the rabbinical theology which Paul constructed in his letter to the Romans and of what Augustine distilled from it: original sin, the absolute necessity of baptism, and the damnation of unbaptized children.

This unhistorical character applies also to the stories in the Book of Exodus about the exodus from Egypt and the entrance into the Promised Land. These stories also were first handed down in oral tradition, and that makes an historian *a priori* suspicious. But there are also solid proofs of their unhistorical character. First, the logistical impossibility referred to already of keeping two to three million people and their cattle alive for 40 years in the desert (cf. the numbers in Exodus 12:37-38). Second, the results of excavations in the last 25 years which show that nothing in the stories fits in with the archaeological evidence. It is true that in the 8th century we find in the prophets Amos and Osee traces of a tradition which knows of an exodus from Egypt and a 40-year journey through the desert. But this tradition can easily be explained as the memory of a limited immigration of an Israelite group from Egypt into Canaan, which had long since been inhabited by Israelites. This immigration – clearly of the tribe of Levi to which Moses and Aaron belonged – would therefore have made up a tiny historical core of the epic stories which were finally written down in the Bible in the 7th century. The exodus from Egypt is therefore not history in the modern sense but a creative epic based on age-old traditions. That applies then both to Yahweh's reaction to the oppression of Israel and to the rescue of little Moses and to his experience at the burning bush (the famous "I am who am" is then the creation of a deeply religious author 600 years later), his mission, the ten plagues, the Easter lamb, the crossing of the Red Sea, the water from the rock, the manna, the quails, the proclamation of the ten commandments, etc. It is good to be aware of this.

The excavations have also consigned to the realm of legend much that is related in the 1st and 2nd Books of Samuel about the early days of the kings. The archaeological discoveries teach us that Jerusalem up to 900 BC, i.e. the time of David and Solomon, was only a large fortified settlement and not the capital city of an imposing kingdom. Added to this is the fact that in contemporary documents, for instance in the Babylonian clay tablets and in Egyptian diplomatic correspondence, there is no trace of the two kings who are so dominant in the Bible. David is clearly not much more than a successful guerrilla fighter who later became a mythical figure and grew considerably in stature at the hands of the biblical authors in the 7th century. The promise to David, which was attributed to God, that his throne, i.e. his dynasty would last forever is the fruit of a nationalistic illusion, the creators and at the same time the victims of which were the biblical authors.

For the liturgy, the Easter liturgy above all, this change of perspective has profound consequences. What is left of the Easter Night ceremonies if there was no exodus as the Bible described it and therefore no "Holy Night", no Pascal meal with unleavened bread, no crossing of the Sea of Reeds (which later changed into the Red Sea)? And we can also forget the pillar of cloud by day and the pillar of fire by night, the making of the covenant on Mount Sinai, the 40 years in the desert, the copper snake, the manna, the quail, and the water from the rock, and so much more that is taken up into the New Testament. However, the liturgy treats Easter as the "fulfilment" of what was predicted in a kind of secret language in the legends narrated in Exodus and Numbers, and it thinks that we will really be penetrated by the Easter message when we share in the (in fact imaginary) experiences of Israel. Therefore in praise of the Easter candle it sings: "The holy festival of Easter has come, at which the true lamb was slaughtered, whose blood makes holy the doors of the faithful and saves the people from death and ruin. This is the night which freed our fathers, the sons of Israel, from Egypt and led them on a dry path through the waves of the Red Sea. This is the night in which the shining pillar drove out the darkness of sin." Then after this praise of the candle, the most important of the seven readings of the service follows: the reading about the crossing of the Red Sea which, by command from above, may under no circumstances be omitted. But also the Jewish Passover no longer has any foundation. It is no longer any kind of actualizing *memoria*, not a memory that makes the past into something in the present, but only a revitalization of legends and no more a *memoria* than, for example, the celebration of the rescue of Isaac in the Islamic Feast of the Sacrifice.

Anyone who knows that cycle of legends can appreciate the exodus stories in the Easter liturgy as language rich in imagery relating to a crucial salutary event in our own lives which has its origin in the ultimate self-surrender of Jesus of Nazareth. The language of images enriches, adds colour, opens up insights. But we have to overlook in our reading much that is savage, and we must not think of the suffering that the ten plagues brought on the poor proletariat on the land in Egypt, of the death of the first-born son in each family, "down to the son of the slave woman kneeling at the hand mill", or of the drowning of the many young soldiers in the waves which suddenly broke over them.

Still more problematic is the fact that the average believer is so unfamiliar with the Bible that he hardly knows anything about the exodus myth. Comparisons are no help where the object with which a comparison is made is itself unknown. And there is no sense in undertaking the time-consuming attempt to familiarize the faithful with a legend which is 2500 years old with a view to illustrating – by what they have learnt on such a detour – the key experience of our faith, which is Easter. It seems more sensible to evoke the richness of that event we call the "resurrection" of Jesus with the aid of modern images, comparisons and stories; in other words, despite all the prophecies of doom of the friends of the Easter liturgy, we should develop a new Easter liturgy. For not the liturgy itself is the aim but the access which it should open for us to a deepened belief in Jesus and in his God.

How did the Torah of the Jews become the Christians' Holy Scripture?

The above is not meant as an attempt to put paid to the Holy Scripture of the Jews. It is only meant to show how unfitting it is to accept uncritically the continually repeated claim that the words of the Bible are the words of God-in-Heaven. The modern Christian believer can do nothing but reject such a claim. Yet that Jewish sacred book remains important also for modern Christians, at least when it is purified of everything that presupposes interventions from a world outside the cosmos. In saying this we are announcing a tentative and still limited rehabilitation of the Old Testament. But this will only be done in detail in the next chapter. First we need to consider the question of how the holy Scriptures of the Jews were, from the beginning, taken to be Holy Scripture for the Christians: in other words, as a true reflection of God's words.

This is simply explained by the fact that the later church followed the lines drawn by the early church, which uncritically saw the Jewish Bible as its own Sacred Scripture. They were Jews and therefore gave credence to the legend that the writer Esra, inspired by the spirit of God, was, after the exile, supposed to have dictated to 40 scribes all the Torah scrolls which had been destroyed by fire in 587 BC. In this way the conviction which had gradually developed before the exile became established – that the Torah originated from Yahweh word for word. Above we tried to explain the development of this conviction as a psychological process which began in Juda with revering this epic as the book of life of the Jewish people. And since this people was the chosen people of Yahweh the content was seen as having Yahweh's blessing and guarantee and was thereby absolutely reliable. That gave the Torah a halo, made it inviolable and sacred. There was a second contributing factor: namely, the authority of the words of the prophets contained in the Bible. Prophets were considered to be mouthpieces of God. About 350 times in the books which bear their name the solemn statement "word of the Lord" occurs. Moses, too, was a prophet and according to Deuteronomy 34,10 even the greatest of them all. Thus the whole Pentateuch, attributed to Moses, was seen as "the word of Yahweh".

Even when the early church began to move away from Judaism it saw no reason to revise its ideas. Hence the Jewish Holy Scripture remained for it, too, the word of God. Added to this was the fact that the divine authority of the Bible was very useful to the early church in its proclamation that Jesus really was the Messiah of God and that his church was the continuation of the old people of God. From its point of view Jesus had been announced in the Old Testament and the prophecies about the Messiah were fulfilled in his life and death. Like a refrain the sentence recurs in the gospels: "So that the Scriptures might be fulfilled." And in the same spirit Luke (24:27) has Jesus explain to the disciples on the road to Emmaus everything that was written about him in the whole of Scripture, "beginning with Moses and all the prophets". The help of the Old Testament was indispensable especially for the Passion story, for Jesus' death on the cross was a great scandal. It seemed to be a complete contradiction of the proclamation that precisely Jesus was the Messiah and the beloved Son of God. A crucified person was in every respect accursed and a reprobate. But it was possible to appeal, for example, to the fourth song of the suffering Servant of God in Isaiah 53 or to Psalm 22, in which the one seemingly abandoned by God triumphs in the end. It seems that the evangelists have even to some extent manipulated the Passion story and fitted the facts to the so-called prophecies, adding details to reinforce the case.

The liturgy and the fathers of the church later interpreted many more texts in this way. If, with tradition, we assume that the Holy Spirit inspired the biblical authors with words and images to support the Christian preachers' arguments there is no problem with interpretations of this kind. But anyone who sees in the Torah an epic of the Jewish people written in the 7th century can only see in it inlaying art, for it is only too clear – something that the pre-modern reader missed – how invented the links between the Old and the New Testament are. Take, for example, the famous passage from Isaiah 7:14: "The young woman (which is in the original) will conceive and bear a son." This text is the prophecy of an event which should serve as a sign to King Achaz. He will therefore have to see it with his own eyes. Therefore it cannot refer to something which will only happen 800 years later. Such a procedure lifts the text out of its context and gives it a meaning which is quite different from the one the (human!) author had in mind. That is not honest.

The notion of fulfilment naturally presupposes that the words of the Torah from time to time (for only seldom does its content lend itself to a Christian interpretation) are of a prophetic nature. But the authors of the Torah were definitely concerned with things quite different from what would happen to Jesus. From the traditional point of view that makes absolutely no difference, for what they wanted to say themselves is completely incon-sequential: the true content of their words is what God wants to communicate through these words. But how can we know that in particular words of a biblical author a message is hidden which is different from the one he intended and that in this way he has become for a moment a divine ventriloquist's puppet? By the so-called fulfilment of the prophecy? But what is called fulfilment can just as much be a chance match or the result of the similarity of the situation in both cases. Or even purely literary imagination, as in 1 Corinthians 10:1-4, where events in Exodus like being under a pillar of cloud, drinking water out of a rock and eating manna are interpreted by Paul as images pointing to baptism and the Eucharist. There are things to be gained from such creative interpretation. But it was hardly the intention of the author of Exodus to teach us, centuries in advance, about the Christian sacraments. But the possibility of parallels with the New Testament are not limited to texts of the Old Testament. When Plato, in the second book of his *Politeia*, speaks about the absolutely just man who will be tortured and crucified, can we say that the Holy Spirit had Plato – without his suspecting it – foretell the death of Jesus on the cross? Plato is merely formulating his insight into the fate awaiting an absolutely just man in an unjust world. And Jesus was such an absolutely just man.

From this the church developed the idea of a *sensus plenior*, or "fuller meaning". This idea means that a deeper meaning is often to be found hidden in a text, a kind of secret divine code which can be read with the help of the Holy Spirit if one eagerly and devotedly enough ponders those words of God. Many authors in the early church, like Origen and later Augustine,were astonishingly creative in this regard. We must admit that the *sensus plenior* found in this way is often a joy and an enrichment. But the danger is always lurking that the message intended by the biblical author disappears in the mist and all that remains is what someone, by means of a supposed revelation from the Holy Spirit, extracts as a hidden meaning but which is really put into the text by the interpreter himself.

From the Jewish Bible to the Christian New Testament

After some time Christians began to see some of their own texts as also inspired. Perhaps this can be explained as follows: these texts reflected the Christian message which ultimately had had its origin in Jesus. In these could be heard, directly or indirectly, the voices of the apostles who had seen and heard Jesus himself and could therefore give first-hand witness to him. Paul also joined the apostles through a back door. And because Jesus had spoken and acted in the name of God and with God's inspiration, the writings which contained his message were also considered to be texts inspired by God and were taken to be God's words. But the border between divine inspiration and divine speech is not clear-cut. And if an author was not one of the apostles (which is mostly the case) it was at least someone, it was thought, who had heard the apostles either with his own ears or through others. Probably that is why tradition teaches that "revelation" – and included in this will be the totality of the writings considered to be inspired – ends with the death of the last apostle. But in fact most of the New Testament authors had their knowledge of Jesus' message not even at second hand, but even third or fourth. The erroneous opinion that the biblical authors were themselves apostles or, like Mark and Luke, had their message directly from an apostle they knew personally explains, for example, that the letter of Clement in the year 90 – which is therefore older than John's gospel – does not belong to Holy Scripture, because it does not come from an apostle, whereas the second letter of Peter does belong to Holy Scripture although it originates from the second century and therefore could not have been written by Peter. He was erroneously considered to be its author only on the basis of the literary fiction in the opening verse that he had written it. The authors would certainly not have suspected that their human words would soon be treated as the words of almighty God. This would have filled them with terror.

In the 4th century a series of such devotedly preserved writings was brought together to form a collection of books considered inspired, and since then they constitute the Bible canon. A canon is a rule which one has to observe, and a list which may not be altered. It is unclear why the Bible canon is comprised of precisely these books, why, in other words, precisely these are considered inspired word-for-word – therefore to be seen as the word of God – and others not. For the letters, the opinion that the author was an apostle played a decisive role. For other writings, especially the gospels, the decisive factors were their early dissemination and the fact that readings from them were used by the communities. The many apocryphal gospels, on the other hand, were eliminated from the canon because their tendency and their spirit were not in tune with the four canonical gospels.

Although the New Testament has the same pre-modern intellectual horizon as the Old Testament and is full of memories of the Torah it cannot simply be tarred with the same brush as the Old Testament. With the use of certain texts from the Torah or the Koran it would be easy to find justification for immoral behaviour, violence, and cruelty. That applies especially to the ten narrative books of the Old Testament. In the Psalms as well we read regrettable evidence of revenge and ruthlessness, as at the end of Psalm 149 which Oliver Cromwell used to give the appearance of religious justification to the slaughtering of his royalist opponents and of the Irish Catholics. Or the well-known Psalm 2, applied to Jesus in the New Testament, according to which God's Anointed would rule the heathens with an iron hand and, if need be, smash them like earthen pots. Not to mention the imprecatory psalms. That the Koran can also be used to justify immoral violence and cruelty needs no further proof today. But precisely the New Testament cannot be used in this way.

The New Testament is not simply the word of God

For a modern believer for whom there is no longer any shuttle service between heaven and earth this statement is clear from the beginning. But it can also be proven *a posteriori*, for exactly as is the case with the Torah the New Testament includes numerous contradictions, impossibilities, improbabilities and even occasionally a statement which one would have to reject on ethical grounds.

There are *contradictions*, for example, between the flight from Bethlehem into Egypt (Matthew 2:14) and the return from Jerusalem to Nazareth (Luke 2:39); or between Jesus' family tree in Matthew 1 and his family tree in Luke 3; or between the apparitions of the risen Jesus in Luke (in his gospel and in the Acts of the Apostles), namely only in Jerusalem, and in Mark and Matthew, namely only in Galilee; or between the dating of Jesus' ascension into heaven in Luke (on Easter day itself) and in the Acts of the Apostles (40 days after Easter); or between blaming Adam in the letter to the Romans 5:17 and Eve in 1 Timothy 2:14. There are also many *impossibilities*, at least in the eyes of a scientifically thinking person: for example, a conception without sperm; stars guiding the way; and other mythological elements in the gospels dealing with Jesus' childhood; miracles in nature, such as the multiplication of the loaves, walking on water and raising from the dead a person in whom putrefaction has already set in. Amongst the *improbabilities* is the chaotic mass migration which the otherwise so practical Romans are supposed to have instigated to organize a census to review taxation. Here Luke is attempting to justify placing the birth of Jesus in Bethlehem. Another case is the content of the conversation between Jesus and Nicodemus and between Jesus and the Samaritan woman (where no disciple was present); or the two long farewell speeches of Jesus at the Last Supper – four chapters in length – of course not written down by anyone and yet communicated to us 60 years later by the fourth evangelist, and in reality thought up by him. *Ethically* blameworthy is the latent anti-Judaism in John, or the vigorous generalizing condemnations of the Scribes and Pharisees in Matthew 23 and Luke 11.

All of this and still much more remains in the shadows as a result of the general conviction that the Bible, including the New Testament, is the "word of the living God". It is astonishing how even highly educated people lose all critical sense as soon as something untenable is put before them backed by a reference to divine authority. Suddenly they then try, often with great acumen, to defend communications supposed to have been rained down from heaven, instead of considering how these things can have meaning and a place in the world in which we live. One can understand the annoyance of militant atheists like Dawkins, Hitchens or Harris when confronted with this sad capitulation of human reason.

There is in addition the fact that the traditionally thinking church treats some of the so-called words of God as human words which are not to be taken very seriously. This applies not only to most of the Old Testament prescriptions, even the most important of them, but also to some in the New Testament, as where Jesus prohibits swearing oaths (the church authorities often require an oath as a means later to enforce obedience), or a repeated admonition to beware of riches or not to resist injustice, or also prescriptions later attributed (but probably later inserted into 1 Corinthians 11) about the head covering of women at gatherings of the faithful. Why should only these words be considered as words of human beings?

The doubts formulated and justified above about the saving force which should come from reading the Old Testament apply equally to the New Testament. As a rule, most of the texts taken from Paul's epistles, for example, mean nothing at all to the faithful at Sunday Mass. They tolerate them as a part of liturgical custom and calmly let them float over their heads. The same applies also to the gospel texts which are not simply narrative. And in any case, reading and hearing the Bible are not absolutely necessary for living as a believer. Many a keen reciter of the rosary does not even own a New Testament or ever open it. And the pious Middle Ages – and they lasted for many centuries – knew almost only the chapters relating to Jesus' childhood and the Passion story, which were to be found everywhere in the so-called "Poor Man's Bible". Clearly, for a 1000 years contact with the rest of the Bible had no relevance to faith.

In summary it can be said that the New Testament is also not words of God that came streaming down from the skies. For modern believers that was already *a priori* clear, for it pre-supposes a division of reality into two separate worlds, deprives the real world of its voice and hands people over to those who claim to be empowered by God-in-Heaven to rule over others. Sacred books belong essentially to religious thinking, to religion. And modernity has taken its leave of religion. Quite rightly so, as is to be explained again in the final chapter of this book. The New Testament is also human language. Martin Luther, who belonged to the late Middle Ages and whose piety was pre-modern, did not yet see this, and so he based the rest of his life on words from Paul in chapter 3:27-28 of the letter to the Romans, that faith alone (but what did Paul mean by this word?) brings justification, and indeed without "works". For him that was an infallible word of God and therefore divine truth, although James in his letter – and this too is infallible divine truth – said that faith (and what did James mean by this word?) without works is dead (2:14). This relativizing of the New Testament words applies also, of course, to the sentence in the fourth gospel: "And the Word was God", which is, by the way, a misleading translation of the Greek original; the correct translation should be: "And the Logos was divine". But how could the evangelist have known what he said about a Logos belonging to God? And yet circumstances have dictated that this human expression originating from the early 2nd century became the foundation stone of the Nicaean creed and of Christian doctrine and has remained such down to the present day.

Chapter Four

Rehabilitation of the Bible

The previous chapter emphasized that the Bible cannot be called "the word of the living God" in the sense that it is comes from God word-for-word. But if not, is it still important for us? More important than other human words, than other books? What follows here is an attempt to show that despite our previous critical analysis it remains very important. This is therefore an attempt to rehabilitate it.

All kinds of arguments are used to defend the Bible. For example, that it has modelled the West and that the West, for its part, has shaped world history in the last five hundred years. That is supposed to prove the importance of the Bible. But the fact is that that influence is derived less from the real biblical message than from the Enlightenment, Western technology, and colonial politics – and these have little to do with that message and to a large extent contradict it. Western culture is undoubtedly indebted to what is good in the Bible, but also to what is less good in it. We need only to think of the discrimination against the non-Jewish world which is seen throughout the whole of the Old Testament; of the anti-Judaism in the New Testament which produced antisemitism and thereby shared responsibility for the Holocaust; of the diminished importance of women in both the Old and the New Testaments; or the biblical fundamentalism which drives the Republicans in the US and the orthodox Jews in Israel – with all the well-known problems it brings for the Near East and the whole world. Perhaps there is a link between, on the one hand, the fact that our Christian West, as a matter of course, goes to war completely against the spirit of its gospels and, on the other hand, the natural acceptance of war in the narrative books of the Torah.

There is also the argument we often hear about the literary value of the Old Testament. It may be a book with often gripping stories and profound reflections, but there are other and even greater literary masterpieces; then, especially in the Old Testament, along with passages of high quality there are others which are boring and arid: for example, the lists of names, enumerations, exact regulations for sacrifice, legal prescriptions. And the New Testament, although it is considered to be the more important part of the Bible, seldom shows literary mastery. Quite honestly, we can forget the literary argument. And even if the Bible were a supreme literary masterpiece, that would be no reason to weigh up each of its golden words – and, above all, no reason to accept each statement as unquestionable truth.

Even the argument that the Bible contains the best news which humanity can hear is not convincing. The Old Testament can only really be considered good tidings if it undergoes radical purification. It is best not to draw attention to much of it. And if one praises the New Testament as the best news for humanity, that still does not apply to passages like the eschatological speech of Jesus in Matthew 24 or the fantastic apocalyptic images in the Book of Revelations. Also, the good in the Bible does not justify the custom within the church of using words from the Bible as definitive arguments in discussions about the meaning of life, no more than it explains the holy zeal with which one tries to find out the exact meaning of obscure texts, or the prohibition from Rome against changing one iota of the official translation. All of this bears witness to the conviction that the Bible is not just an extremely important human creation but a collection of words of God-in-Heaven and that therefore every word of this book is infinitely precious and absolutely reliable. But for modernity this conviction has had its day.

A true rehabilitation, at least of the New Testament (rehabilitation of the Old Testament can only come after it) should have as its starting point that it is the written record of the words and actions of the historical Jesus of Nazareth together with the first believers' reflexions of his disciples. For us Christians, this Jesus is of the highest importance and is the object of our veneration – which does not necessarily take the form, as in tradition, of an apotheosis, i.e. of a deification. But the more important *he* is for us, the more important is the New Testament for us, for this book helps us to know this wonderful person who is filled with the divine; it encourages us to turn to him, it provides the foundation of our Christian belief and the options for living which derive from it. At the same time it helps us to recognize it for what it is and to reject everything in today's society that is foreign to this belief: namely, the esotericism, transmigration of souls, polytheism, deism, dialectical materialism, and everything that is foreign to a Christian way of life or clearly contradicts it, like hunger for power, greed, vengefulness or intolerance.

But does that necessarily mean that we go back to the New Testament itself? What we are looking for can surely be found in the Catechism and in the pious books or in theology courses. Even to become familiar with the person of Jesus of Nazareth and with his message it is perhaps better to read a good book about him – and there is a whole host of good books about him – than to try and form a consistent image of him from reading the gospels. All of these books paint a one-sided image of him, one which the author has formed for himself. But even the way each of the four gospels presents Jesus is one-sided. It is the same with the way Paul, John or James think and speak of him in their letters. It is clear from church history that personal reading of or pondering on the New Testament is not absolutely necessary. This has been the experience of the ordinary church members (and these are the Church – more than are the Vatican and all the bishops) over a period of 1000 years. What the faithful knew of the New Testament was limited to what they heard from the pulpit (where there was preaching) or to what they saw in scenes depicted in painting and sculpture in the churches. But ultimately all sermons, depictions and believers' interpretations refer back to the New Testament. This book is and remains the basis for our personal encounter with Jesus of Nazareth and of our proclaiming that he is God's great self-revelation. That makes the New Testament irreplaceable for a Christian and much more important than all literary masterpieces or the Tao, the Vedas or the Bhagavad Gita.

The New Testament as "Word of God"

In the previous chapter it was explained why the expression "word of God" (here we must keep in mind that in this context "word" means "speaking") is anthropomorphic and therefore mythological language. In addition to this, it is quite impossible to prove that human words are in fact also words of the transcendent God. Anyone who, despite everything, maintains this is only copying what others say, and these are copying others, until we come to those who first began to think and announce this.

But how did these latter come to this conviction? The phenomenon of inspiration offers an explanation. The inspired artist is aware that what he writes or composes or paints is not his own autonomous creation. It does come from his own inner depths, but he does not freely and autonomously summon it up. It is, as it were, given to him. It is the fruit of inspiration – literally, a breathing in. When reality is divided into two worlds people spontaneously think of this creative impulse as originating from the other world and being inspired from there. This happens, for example, with a muse, a goddess who speaks through the poet. That is why the *Iliad* begins with a prayer to the Muse: "Sing, Goddess, the terrible anger of Achilles", although Homer himself will sing of this anger and its disastrous consequences in 15,693 verses. The biblical authors had the same experience. They tried to express what slumbered deep within them and wanted to come to light, but because of the Yahwist tradition they experienced this as something inspired in them by Yahweh, as Yahweh speaking in them and through them.

But why did the listeners or readers accept this? Probably because of the stirring power of their message. This power came from the deep wisdom and truth of these words, from their beauty or ethical richness, in short: from the presence of the true, the beautiful and the good, which are some of the so-called "transcendentals", qualities proper to the absolute which as such transcend us. Hence their name. As qualities of the absolute they give us a sense of the inexpressible, which the religions call "God" and to which each religion gives its own content.

The pre-modern interpretation of inspired human words as words from God-in-Heaven is by its very nature mythological and leads to conclusions which were discussed in the previous chapter. We should therefore try to remove talk of the "Word of God" out of its mythological shell and reformulate it in the language of a modern believer.

We can start by saying that the evolving cosmos is self-expression of a nameless spiritual fundamental reality which in this way makes itself visible and audible, expresses itself in the cosmos and, in particular, in man. We call this self-expression creation. It is not static but is in a state of continual evolution. This means that the fundamental reality "expresses itself" gradually more richly in the course of the cosmic aeons, more richly therefore in the *homo sapiens* than in the preceding phases of evolutionary history, and most richly, as the Christian believes, in Jesus of Nazareth. In this sense Jesus is the great self-revelation of God, God's clearest "speech", his "Word" – everything in inverted commas to indicate that this is purely the language of imagery.

What the fundamental reality says and does through Jesus is, however, culturally conditioned. This includes the possibility of culture-related errors and the need for later correction. Take, for example, Jesus' conviction that the end of the existing unjust society and the breakthrough of a new world – which he called the Kingdom of God – was at hand; or his threatening words about the fate of those who did not accept his words. But if certain words or actions of Jesus leave us feeling uneasy, the reason probably lies with his witnesses who spontaneously translated what they heard and experienced into the old way of seeing things and handed it on like this until it found expression in the gospels.

When we encounter Jesus we encounter the clearest self-expression of the unfathomable God. But genuine encounter is always to some extent identification, and identification with the creative fundamental mystery by means of the encounter with Jesus means inner change, growth, and healing development. This change for the good in those who encountered the historical Jesus continues in the words in which they give witness to the encounter. To this extent there is present in these words something of God's creative speaking – in a diluted form as it were – and contact with this speaking brings about change in man for the good. This contact is, of course, not to be understood as the passive or non-comprehending listening to the Scripture reading, to which for most church-goers it is unfortunately reduced. Genuine contact consists in one's feeling "addressed" by what one reads or hears. That proves that one has really heard God speaking. Just as a poet can communicate to his readers or listeners his inner experiences, his "inspiration", with the help of his words, so too can the evangelist communicate to his readers or listeners the inspiration he has experienced through his encounter with the words and actions of Jesus. That this is in fact the case can be seen from the change for the good which takes place in them.

Because the recording of this inspiration is the work of human beings, it also contains ballast, elements which are only too human, conditioned by time, no longer tenable, wrecked notions left behind in the wake of ongoing developments. Instead of enriching us and giving us joy as God's words should do, we are aggravated by them: for example, by the idea of the end of the world, i.e. that the end is imminent; or that the Son of Man is coming on the clouds of heaven; or the narration of miracles which make a joke of the laws of nature; or confusing mythological fantasies as in the letter of Jude or the Book of Revelation; or the rabbinical aspects in several of Paul's arguments. The author is hindered by his own particular limitations from letting the "word of God" that is in him – his contact with the self-communication of God in Jesus – flow down to us in the 21st century. When we come across such texts we are only reading human words.

It follows that the important aspect of contact with the Bible is not found in knowing, and therefore not in exegesis, and still less in knowledge that one can victoriously demonstrate in a Bible quiz, but in feeling "addressed" and in the experiences that follow from this: light, courage, liberation, joy, meaningfulness, peace. Insofar as the New Testament awakens such experiences in us it deserves the name "word of God". And it deserves the name as the record of the encounter with Jesus of Nazareth at that time, in whom the divine mystery is revealed.

Therefore, despite all the ballast, we will do better to pick up the New Testament rather than the Vatican's *Catechism of the Catholic Church*, which is a time-conditioned system bringing the gospel message to us only through the filter of a pre-modern kind of theological discourse.

Limited rehabilitation of the Old Testament

Can we then also see the Old Testament as God's speech? Behind this question lurks the tacit assumption that there is an essential distinction between the two books. But such a distinction is not in line with tradition, which has always upheld the equal status of the two testaments, as many church documents prove. The Second Vatican Council did strike a new note in acknowledging the greater importance of the New Testament. But in this more or less modern council most of the participants still had no problem with treating the "word of God" anthropomorphically and therefore mythologically. In a mode of thinking which is no longer mythological we have to stress the distinction between the Old and the New Testament even more strongly than the council did.

Insofar as Jesus is for us the decisive revelation of God, the New Testament is where we encounter God. On the other hand, the Old Testament is the record of how God was experienced by numerous wise men, prophets and mystics in Israel. The same applies to this record as to that of the New Testament but with two corrections. The encounter with Jesus means a much richer experience than the mystical experience expressed in the Old Testament. But the Old Testament, the Torah, was the fruitful soil which produced Jesus' vision and message. As a revelation of God, Jesus is not a case of *generatio spontanea*. He was spiritually awakened and formed by the divine experience which was recorded in the Torah and which he was able to share in through his familiarity with the Torah. His education initiated him into it. He assimilated it and let himself be led by its inspiration, as is clear from many gospel texts. That is why the Torah is important for us as well.

On the other hand, the Old Testament is by no means a hidden annunciation of Jesus secreted by the Holy Spirit here and there in the words of the unsuspecting authors in the way we hide Easter eggs in the garden for children to find. Jesus of Nazareth was completely unknown to them. Thus we should not look there for any proofs sown by the Holy Spirit that he is the Messiah they hope for. The Old Testament is simply the Holy Scripture of the Jews who have neither found nor inserted in it anything that has to do with Jesus and the Church. Jesus' disciples did use the Old Testament as such a repository of proofs of his messianic calling. Using an extremely limited selection (only very few are suitable) they tried to show their Jewish co-believers that despite his catastrophic end he was still Israel's longed for Messiah. But this church formed by Jews was transformed gradually into a church joined by heathens who had hardly any knowledge of the Old Testament – which then gradually lost this function of proof more and more. It lost it even more, of course, in the transition to modern thinking. Prophecies from on high are seen there as pious fantasy.

Then what does the Old Testament mean for us if it is not a repository of prophecies about Jesus and his church? The record of authentic experiences of God in the lives of many pious Jews. The holy, which will have its breakthrough in Jesus (for the author of the 4th gospel, Jesus is therefore the perfect expression of God, simply God's word), is already expressed there. Thanks to the experiences of God expressed in it God can speak also to us, i.e. reveal and communicate himself. These words can also become "God's words" for us. They can be experienced in the form of inner liberation, enrichment, enlightenment.

But the Old Testament brings with it, as we have said, more and heavier ballast than the New Testament has. It is still partly steeped in a culture of completely primitive elements which the modern believer has largely cast off, as for example the image of Yahweh as a belligerent God, an avenging and punishing God, one who is eager for sacrifice, takes sides, and who sees no problem with executions, punitive expeditions and genocide. This image disappears for the most part in and after the Babylonian exile. But the Torah as a whole is characterized by a Jewish pride (we alone are God's own people, other peoples are in this respect second rank) which causes problems for modern people. The utterances which follow from this – nationalism, desire for vengeance and for power which occur even in the psalms – result in there being in the same measure in many Old Testament passages no longer any mention of encounter with God. Such texts can prove to be fascinating stories, superb poetry, superb literary achievements, but these qualities do not make of the Old Testament a more special place of encounter with God's word than does the *Iliad*.

What is left after this critical analysis? That the Bible can only be seen as God speaking (no longer understood in the mythological sense) insofar as we feel in it "depths" which inspire, enlighten, liberate, and encourage us, make us more creative, more loving, in short: humanize us. God's speech is essentially creative, renewing, aimed at incarnation. All the zeal of the translators, the endless exegetical discussions and the doctoral theses about the exact meaning of texts or sentences – which no believer ever reads but which are part of the ballast we drag along – lose sight of the proper function of Holy Scripture. All of this could be justified earlier by the conviction that in every sentence or even in every word of the Bible we heard God's own voice. Only since, with modernity, we have given up this notion, has the weakness of this blind reverence for the Bible come to light.

Bible texts *are* not, as such, "God speaking" to us; they *become* that insofar as they *address* us in the depths of ourselves. That is what can be expected from God's speaking. It is the intimate speech of one person to another. We sense that it is God who speaks to us in these human words because of the movement they awaken in us to do good, to have more humanity. One conclusion that stands out was already formulated above: we should not read *the* Bible (undifferentiated promotion of Bible reading is "much ado about nothing") but we should read *in* the Bible and, in it, precisely what speaks to and nourishes us, even if this is limited to a tiny fraction of the whole book.

But then there can be many more human words which, apart from the Bible, become "God's words" to us. In the occurrence of every encounter with God his words are present. They are also present in the enriching experiences which we owe to fellow men and events, and definitely also to nature – for here the divine fundamental reality expresses itself in innumerable forms. "Revelation", at least when it refers to God's self-communication and not the totality of messages from God-in-Heaven as pre-modern believers understand it, did not therefore conclude with the death of the last apostle. The exclusiveness of the Bible as "God's words" according to the late Jewish and early Christian and pre-modern belief is to that extent out-of-date.

At the same time we should frankly admit that many Bible texts bring us no nearer to God, and in this sense are not God's words to us. The reason can be the obsolete image of God they contain or our limited familiarity with biblical culture which results in our not understanding or in our misunderstanding the text. Or the reason could be that in general its way of thinking and articulating is alien to people living in the 21st century. In the age in which these texts were written the language was probably the best there was and was clear to everyone, and was to this extent "word of God" for them, but this is no longer the case for us.

Conclusion

Examined more closely, tradition reveres the Bible in exactly the same way as Islam reveres the Koran. For the Muslim believer this too contains the perfect truth because it is the pure word of Allah, which, untouched and unchanged, came to Mohammed through Gabriel and then through Mohammed to us. Koran criticism is thereby for Islam essentially unbelief. Bible criticism was also for a long time considered as unbelief. Only after tough resistance and after many condemnations did the Church, under pressure from irrefutable modern arguments, make room for Bible criticism and then even admit the need for it. But Bible criticism treats Bible texts as human words, and human words can and should be laid on the dissecting table. But is it possible and allowable also to put God's words on the dissecting table? One can only accept them reverently and try to understand them as they are! This is what the Muslims do with the words of the Koran. But while the Church authorities accept Bible criticism and therefore to that extent treat the Bible as human words it remains inconsistent and stresses that Scripture is simply the "word of the living God", as it requires the readers to proclaim after every reading from the Old and the New Testament. The two chapters devoted to the Bible in this book have tried to show what the modern believer can retain.

Briefly it is this: what is very anthropomorphically called "Word (really: speaking) of God" is not so much a collection of written signs in a book as an activity. It is first and foremost the evolving self-expression of God in an evolving cosmos, culminating in the person of Jesus of Nazareth. We encounter this Jesus in the New Testament, especially in the gospels. These are a record of the experience of God (which is the human side of God's self-communication) by a group of people who met Jesus and were impressed by him. In this record we encounter in the most striking way the creative Fundamental Love, God, which is revealed most clearly in the shape of Jesus of Nazareth. Precisely this is what constitutes the unique value of the New Testament.

But also in the experiences of the divine in the lives of the authors of the Torah, which is the source of Jesus' own experience of God, we can hear God speaking. The fact that it is God speaking through their experiences, i.e. that it is really God we encounter in their words, will show itself in the humanizing change which takes place in us. The same applies to the New Testament. If these words change nothing in us, if everything remains as it was, we have only heard human words and not words of God. No matter how much we incense the book, kiss it reverently, and carry it with solemnity through the church – that is all nothing more than a ritual performance.

Chapter Five

But Why Annoy Us with That "Holy Mass"?

Just as with the title of Chapter Four there is a slight annoyance here. The annoyance is now no longer that of the free spirits, since they only shrug at the ritual procedure, but that of a believer who finds that "Holy Mass" has become a tenacious ivy which overruns Christian existence on all sides. The facts clearly support this opinion. To be a Catholic is largely identified with "going to Sunday Mass". Clearly, shameless greed, racism, a life without prayer or without social commitment, without willingness to forgive – these are far less incompatible with being a Christian than staying away from Sunday Mass. Also, no single Catholic "event" is conceivable without the most solemn possible celebration of Mass. This applies to jubilees, Papal visits, World Youth Days, trips to Rome, canonizations, funerals, confirmations, weddings. Canon law moves in the same groove by insisting that priests celebrate Mass every day and that members of religious communities receive the Eucharist every day, i.e. seven times as often as the average churchgoer. The First Holy Communion is an enormous feast for the child's family and parish even if the parents afterwards (and perhaps even beforehand) hardly ever set foot in the church, and after the first communion of the child a second one will scarcely follow. In most parishes even on the first Sunday after this inflated event there will hardly be any first communicant in the church. What is so important about the Mass and Communion that they have taken over such a dominant role in the Roman Catholic Church?

The answer is given indirectly in the title of the Synod of Bishops 2005 taken from the Papal letter *Sacramentum Caritatis*: "Eucharist, Source and Highlight of the Whole Life of the Christian". The word "source" suggests that without the Mass the life of Christians would die of thirst. And "highlight" infers that for Catholics participation in the celebration of Mass is a crowning event by comparison with all else. The title of that Synod of Bishops is taken from the constitution *Lumen Gentium* of the Second Vatican Council and contains still more statements exalting the Eucharist: for example, the church lives and grows by it unceasingly, it is the realization of the unity of the faithful, in it the fellowship with Christ and with one another comes about. Is this really so?

What does Holy Scripture say about this?

When we open the Scripture to see what the early Church thought, the Eucharist did not seem so eminently important. The oldest witness, Paul, mentions it only in 1 Corinthians 10 and 11. This means that of the c. 180 columns which make up his authentic letters as well as others attributed to him not even two are devoted to it. For Paul the emphasis lies on justification, on the bond which God gives us with himself. For Paul the genuine source of life for the Christian is faith, not as an intellectual act but as a surrender of the heart. Moreover, those two columns from 1 Corinthians contain no call to frequent participation in the Eucharist; instead there are warnings and threats in relation to it. At the beginning of chapter 10 Paul recalls some of the (for us legendary) events which took place in the desert in the exodus from Egypt. He sees them as prefigurations of the (only) two sacraments there were at that time: baptism and Eucharist, and he states that these, of themselves, do not at all have a saving function – by contrast to faith and doing the will of God. And in 11:29-30 he describes first what Jesus said and did at the Last Supper, adding that participation at this remembrance is, for many, a source of doom rather than salvation. His other statements about the Eucharist are limited to two references connected with his criticism of eating the flesh of animals sacrificed in honour of idols. All of this does not amount to much. At any rate there is nothing in Paul's writings about "source" and "highlight".

The synoptic evangelists writing after him relate, in the context of the Passion story, the events at the Last Supper, the so-called institution narrative. Here there is no further mention of the Eucharist. In Mark and Matthew there is no instruction to repeat later, in his memory, what he has done, i.e. to celebrate the Eucharist. Thus we cannot speak of an institution narrative in their gospels. We find this instruction only in Paul and in Luke, who on this point is dependent on him. In the fourth evangelist there is not even the story of the ritual with bread and wine. Clearly he considers service more important than this rite. It is thought that in chapter 6 we find a text which is central for understanding the Eucharist. But, as we now need briefly to show, this chapter of John's gospel, despite the vocabulary used, is not dealing with the Eucharist but with faith in Jesus. This faith is the "source" of our thinking and living as Christians.

A careful reading reveals, namely, that the content from verse 29 onwards is a call to such faith, for through it we take Jesus existentially into ourselves, let ourselves be taken over and fulfilled by him, become new human beings and begin to live, really to live, to live eternally. The three formulations: come to Jesus, believe in him and eat him as if he were bread clearly mean in v.35 the same. It continues in this vein without reference to the Eucharist, until suddenly, in vv. 51b-56 we read that we are to eat Jesus' flesh and drink his blood – and that refers to the Eucharist, does it not? These six verses interrupt the flow of thought and give the impression that they are an insert, for up to 51a the text is concerned exclusively with faith in Jesus referred to by the author by using the symbol of eating, as if Jesus were bread. Also in the summary at the end, Jesus' sermon, constructed by the author, only deals with this faith, as if up to this point no other theme had been dealt with.

What those six verses promise as fruit of the eating and drinking, namely, eternal life, has already been promised in exactly the same words in v. 40 as fruit of faith in Jesus. This (material) eating and drinking achieves nothing that has not already been achieved through faith. Such eating and drinking is therefore nothing more than symbolic language expressing this faith. One can furthermore ask whether the use of this almost brutal symbolic language was a fortunate choice by the author. It is hardly conceivable that Jesus himself would have spoken like this. We only need to think of the repeated prohibition of blood consumption in the Torah (Leviticus 17:10-14 for example) and the worldwide condemnation of cannibalism. We can only wonder how these verses came into the text and, equally, why the Church has had no problem with them down to the present day. Probably the conviction, in tradition, that every word in the gospel comes from God cancels out our spontaneous unease. And experience teaches us that formulae which we have heard from early childhood do not disturb us. But anyone who hears for the first time that he has to eat the flesh of Jesus and drink his blood can only be shocked and baulk at it.

What do we learn from observation and from history?

Apart from the passages quoted, the New Testament has nothing at all to say about the Eucharist. What was the basis, therefore, for the Second Vatican Council's maintaining that the Eucharist should be the source and highlight of our lives as Christians? Perhaps it was the experience that the Eucharist has had in the past and still has today such a radical and beneficial influence on the life of Christians? In other words, does experience teach us that the Council's statement was correct? Unfortunately not. To begin with, there are the hundreds of millions of Christians of the Reformation for whom this is not the case. For them the source is "God's word" to us, although they have identified this one-sidedly and in a completely pre-modern way with the words of the Bible.

But also for the average Catholic the Eucharist is, in reality, not a source and highlight of his life as a Christian. Most Sunday churchgoers experience there not only no highlight but as a rule nothing at all. If they did experience something sublime and rich and nourishing their numbers would not have shrunk to a tenth in fifty years. People perform their Sunday duty, preferably at a distance from the altar and piously, and indifferently, let the liturgical process pass over them. If this Sunday ritual is for those present the highlight of their lives as Christians what is the rest of it like? This Sunday Mass also changes nothing in their behaviour, which challenges its character as a source. The rite also does not weld them together. They prefer not to sit too close to strangers and at the end of the celebration they do not look for contact. Yet according to Paul 1 Corinthians 10:15 they are "one body" by eating from the one bread. When the bishops in the Council declared that the Eucharist is the accomplishment of the unity of the faithful and that in it the fellowship with Christ and with one another is realized, they had probably never experienced any normal Sunday Mass in a country parish.

Another indication that this glorifying language is pure idealization is the usual way of speaking about the Sunday duty.

What has to be done under threat of hell and damnation (as it was preached from the pulpit for hundreds of years) can hardly count as source and highlight. If the Eucharist were really to be experienced as a highlight in the faithful's experience, the Sunday churchgoers might be expected to appear at Mass also on weekdays. But that seldom happens.

Such an intensive experience, a highlight, should have a powerful effect on the rest of the day. But even with pious people memory of the celebration of Mass plays no further part in the day. Was that any different for the bishops who, during the Synod, exchanged their ideas at length about the Eucharist as "source and highlight"? Were they formulating their own experiences or were they just duly repeating the Council's sentence with (unconscious?) conformism? The bishops do tend to have no problem with simply repeating further statements which critical historical thinking has shown to be untenable. For example, that they are the successors of the apostles, which Adolf von Harnack completely disproved a hundred years ago; that the pope is the successor of Peter; that the seven sacraments were instituted by Jesus; or that outside of the (Roman Catholic?) Church there is no salvation.

If "Holy Mass" for most churchgoers has more value in comparison to a word or prayer service with or without Communion, this is often attributed to the opinion that in their eyes a "genuine" Mass – one with the "consecration" – liberates a soul from purgatory. Of course, this has little to do with events at the Last Supper, where there was no mention at all of souls and purgatory. Here, the reason for the believers' mistaken notion is the interpretation of the Eucharist as a sacrifice, i.e. as a gift which we offer to God to get something from him on the principle *do ut des*: I am giving you a gift, so that you will give me a gift. What is called a high point clearly is reduced in this perspective to a medium of exchange with which we can do something for the "poor souls in purgatory". Does that mean that we can order and pay for sources and high points?

History also contradicts that idealizing view of the Second Vatican Council and of the Synod of Bishops. In the course of the Middle Ages and of the Counter Reformation billions of Masses were "said". This enormous flood should have improved the lives of people in the West in a wonderful way, first of all by powerfully promoting love for one another. But what do we see?

For mass-goers it was public entertainment to witness how one's fellow men were cruelly killed in the market place, broken on the wheel, flayed, immersed in boiling water, quartered; how the use of torture to extract a confession was a normal part of the judicial system, without theologians who celebrated daily Mass or pious judges protesting against this inhuman abuse; how the intensely pious but at the same time equally intensely avaricious Spaniards in Latin America had no scruples about enslaving the Indians and torturing them to death, taking their land and plundering it so that they could decorate their churches with the silver and gold they stole, and celebrate there "the source and highlight of their lives as Christians"; how very Catholic princes who would never have missed Sunday Mass continuously waged war, which always involved murder, rape, plundering and destruction, and robbed the poor of the little they had as a basis for living; how the prisons were worse than disgusting, the number of starving beggars was huge and the living conditions of serfs were pitiable. In the face of all this the Church leaders, who perhaps said Mass every day, were outrageously rich. Would it have been still worse if fewer Masses had been said? The question is whether it *could* have been worse. Nothing of all this fits together with faith in God and in Jesus, since the content of faith is that one allows oneself to be swayed by love and consequently by human sympathy.

"Holy Mass" above all a religious ritual

A third objection against the view shared by the Council and the Synod is based on the idea that "Holy Mass" is a ritual. Nothing against rituals! They are good in themselves and we cannot do without them. Our life is full of them: the applause after a performance, rules of ceremony, a handshake on meeting, burial customs, requirements regarding clothing, the demands of etiquette, and much more. The explanation of this multiplicity certainly does not lie in the usefulness of rituals: they have no use. They are essentially non-useful. They are not a means to achieve something else. Perhaps it is this lack of usefulness that explains their success. By doing this useless thing a person breaks through the naked objectivity of his existence and achieves a minimal experience of transcendence. We need such experiences. This can also explain the experience of security which is bound up with participation in rituals. It also explains the binding character associated with rituals. For rituals are simply there. They are not a free creation of the individual in the present moment. They come therefore from elsewhere, in a certain sense from above. The prescribing "above", however, can also be a super-ego, built into us by the group or society to which we belong and can therefore present us with an appearance of transcendence.

All of this applies also to *religious* rituals. They raise the otherwise nameless presence of the transcendent into our consciousness. In other words, they deal expressly with God. *Christian* rituals, for their part, give this presence a specific content characterized by the quite particular conception of God which the Christian community has inherited from Jesus. The Roman Catholic rituals interpret this Christian notion of God in their own specific way which is influenced more by popular piety than by inherited Christian substance. Of these Catholic (and Orthodox) rituals "Holy Mass" has become quite simply *the* ritual. Its ritual and strictly binding character is revealed quite clearly by the fact that higher authority again and again reminds us that nothing can be altered in the content or execution of the Mass. In the earlier Moral Theology text-books every significant departure from these prescriptions was even considered a mortal sin.

But it is not possible for a ritual to be the supreme realization of our lives as Christians, still less its source. It belongs to the realm of signs, i.e. of symbolic expressions, whereas being a Christian belongs to the existential domain, i.e. to the reality which has to do with the inner process of becoming one with God. Signs, on the other hand, can be mere appearance and misleading. The designation "highlight of Christian life" is deserved therefore much more by the human compassion of a social worker in Ecuador who, despite death threats, continues his commitment to the repressed Indians. A ritual can indeed help us to give tangible shape to our personal turning to the God who is Fundamental Love, and to make us more sympathetic. For signs are also creative. They realize to some extent what they signify. A ritual is therefore to that extent an aid to Christian life, and this applies also to the Eucharist. As a ritual it is then a source like other sources such as reading, conversation, prayer, commitment to fellow men. Perhaps it is a richer source, but it is not *the* source.

Rituals are also characterized by repeatability. They cry out for repetition since we want to experience the minimal transcendence experience anew. But too great frequency without change (and the fact that the rituals are already there allows very little room for variations) brings with it the great danger of getting into a rut, and this is lethal for the expressive quality of a sign and therefore for the creative force of the ritual. Therefore praise and also the requirement of daily Eucharist for the clergy and members of religious orders is a very dubious thing. This frequency threatens to hollow out the Eucharist, reduce it to the level of a harmless pious custom and rob it of its inner force. And can remembrance of Jesus' behaviour at the Last Supper survive such continual repetition? Probably no more than daily repetition of the Stations of the Cross.

Relativity of the sacramentals

The specifically Catholic (and Orthodox) rituals are called sacramentals. They are characterized by the fact that they make something material into an incarnation of the divine, into a place for making contact with the holy. Anyone who defiles this material thing, for example by smashing a statue of a saint or trampling on hosts, defiles something holy, commits a sacrilege. The Catholic community has many sacramentals: signing with ashes, washing of feet, procession with palms, Blasius blessing, incensing, monastic choir-singing, consecration and all kinds of blessings: of candles, medals, holy water, Three Wise Men water, Ignatius water, palms, oil of chrisam, crucifixes and statues of saints, Easter food, Easter candle, churches and altars, etc. The Orthodox Church is also rich in sacramentals, the Reformed churches, on the other hand, much less so.

Anyone who thinks like a modern believer can only relativize the importance and the value of the sacramentals. They are the products of a pre-modern view according to which the cosmos is profane, only potentially holy. It has not in fact become holy, it is not concretely the dwelling place of God and is not the place to find him. For God belongs to another world. He can, in fact, appear in our world, which is potentially holy. But even this he cannot do everywhere. For example, he cannot do it in a relationship between divorced people who have married again, because he condemns them – at least that is what Rome says. What is in itself profane reality can normally be, as it were, elevated to holiness. That is what the sacramentals do. They make a Jacob's ladder out of profane reality, and by means of it they can ascend to God.

In this view of things it is the activity of the Church that makes things holy, for only in this way is God present with his sanctifying influence. Hence a Church official is needed for the consecration or blessing – preferably a priest, or if need be, a deacon, or at least a baptized person. For also a baptized father or a baptized mother is a person of the Church. Through the little cross made on the child's forehead God will become present to the child. Without this cross perhaps God will not protect the child. For that reason it is best to have many and frequent blessings: candles, water, food, statues, mopeds, fire-brigade vehicles – the series is endless. The more blessings and consecrations there are, the more the profane cosmos is made holy. This is the origin of the pious custom to devote the beginning of the day to God and thus to consecrate to him the whole day. Without this consecration it would remain profane, unholy. The tag "holy" is being stuck on the day. But the tag does not change the content. Either the day is holy by virtue of the fundamental God/love being active in it or it remains just as unholy and wretched as before, despite all the tags.

But in these well-meaning consecrations lurks a grave danger. The notion imperceptibly slips in that the consecration or blessing loads the material object with a real force. The crucifix on the wall is to keep disaster at bay, holy water is no longer a reminder of baptism but an efficient means to chase away evil, a Christopher medal or a blessing of the car or the motor-bike will protect the driver/rider from accidents. And immediately we land in the quicksand of superstition and magic.

If the sacramentals, in the pre-modern perspective, have the function of making the cosmos a little bit holy, they should in the view of the modern believer draw attention to the sacred character of the cosmos. They are like light beams which make this holiness light up for a moment. For the cosmos *is* the self-revelation of the holy fundamental reality, the creative love which makes itself visible in all things, driving them to their perfection and driving human beings to complete humanity. Thus the focus shifts from heaven to earth. Action for the reduction of CO_2 emissions, for protection of the rainforests, for limiting the use of energy, for a day off from work on Sundays; actions against nuclear reactors, nature pollution, discrimination (often wrongly called racism), the sending back of refugees who are already integrated – such actions are hardly sacramentals, since non-believers also take part in them. But they are linked with the God preached by Jesus and, by contrast to many sacramentals, are not in danger of sliding into magic or superstition. A solemn consecration of the North Sea or of the Elbe is, from a believer's point of view, less important than action to ensure that the North Sea is not fished empty or that the Elbe is not contaminated. Prayer, reflection, therapeutic fasting, contemplation, even yoga may not be sacramentals, but they are more important than sprinkling holy water or making the sign of the cross.

Relativizing the sacraments

Seven sacramentals have gradually won a special place in the life of the church. To distinguish them from the rest they are called sacraments. According to the Father of the Church, Augustine, in the 5th century *sacramentum* – literally: means of sanctification – was still the name for all that we now call sacramentals. The first two rituals which stood out as especially important are baptism and the Eucharist. The number of rituals with a special status gradually grew until they reached the holy (or magic) number seven. The Council of Trent solemnly teaches that these seven were instituted by Jesus himself. This is what makes them different and gives them their unique value. But here the Council is clearly wrong. The institution by Jesus of the anointing of the sick or the sacrament of marriage is historically not tenable. And why is, for example, the washing of feet which was "instituted" by Jesus (the disciples were to do as he did, he says in John 13:14-15) not a sacrament?

We should question the importance not only of the sacramentals but also that of the sacraments and, along with that, their necessity. The church began quite early to relativize the need for baptism. Originally it considered baptism absolutely necessary for eternal salvation but it gradually diminished this absoluteness first by accepting the "baptism of blood" as equally salutary and then the baptism of desire, even the baptism of implicit desire, and it finally gave up the age-old idea that unbaptized children would have to be satisfied with being in limbo. Now children who die without baptism are not considered to be at a disadvantage compared with the baptized. This retreat is found in practice: the number of unbaptized children in Catholic families is steadily growing, slowly but surely. In any case, most of the baptisms of children are now only religiously coloured birth celebrations in which rebirth out of the water and the Holy Spirit, as the liturgy says of baptism, or the source of eternal salvation are no longer talked about. Thus the demise of child baptism is no great loss. Moreover, for a modern-thinking believer it is clear that the crucial factor is not the baptism ritual but the turning in faith to Jesus and through him to God. It is only this that changes us existentially, gives us "eternal life", saves us. Chapter 6 of John's gospel, referred to above, says it clearly enough. Baptism is at most the symbolical, because ritual, expression of this turning to Jesus. But one can well lead the life of a believer without this symbol. If by chance we had not been "validly" baptized (because certain conditions laid down by Canon Law had not been fulfilled) this would change nothing with regard to our salutary faith.

The ritual which we call "Holy Mass" is also of relative importance in our lives as Christians. The texts prescribed by Rome for this ritual originate from the early Middle Ages and have hardly any relevance to modern believers. For example, in the Eucharistic Prayer, after the consecration the celebrant is meant to pray: "Take this spotless sacrificial gift like the gifts of your just servant Abel and the sacrifice of our father Abraham and the pure sacrifice of your High Priest Melchizedec." Do many believers know what this is about? Do they feel it means something to them? These texts can sound solemn and sublime, and even a splendid festive Mass on television or a Midnight Mass at Christmas can be very moving. But ultimately the Eucharist is not concerned with emotion and aesthetic experience but with renewal which is meant to come about through encounter with Jesus and, through him, with God.

If, on the other hand, the essential thing for us is not this encounter and renewal but an old familiar and comforting ritual – the return to the Latin Mass where the celebrant has his back to the congregation is a symptom of this – then we become guilty of sacralizing and clericalizing our Christian life. Sacralizing, by acting as if one is only a proper Christian if one is concerned with the sacred ceremony instead of with one's fellow men; and clericalizing by making our encounter with the holy dependent on the activity of a priest.

There is yet another reason why we should not expect too much from the sacraments, even from the Eucharist: namely, because modernity lacks the spiritual organ required to experience the sacrament as sacrament, i.e. as an inwardly healing and renewing sign, and therefore more than a holy ritual. The early church still had such an organ. It lived in a cultural climate in which a human activity could be experienced as incarnation and revelation of a divine activity. John's baptism ritual, later taken over by the early church, could be experienced by people as a bath from which one could emerge, as it were, inwardly reborn, as a real purification and renewal brought about by the spirit of God through the ritual. Experiencing this unity of the worldly and the divine is not the same as grasping it intellectually. Today's churchgoers can perhaps still manage the latter, but they can certainly no longer manage the former. That is the price we have to pay for belonging to a technological society, but we should not lose sight of the advantages that this entails. Yet we can still experience something external as an internal event. We have an example of this in marriage vows, which cause an inner change in the couple. We are still aware of inner-worldly symbolism even if to a lesser extent than previously. But it has become virtually impossible for us to experience a human act as divine.

Another difficulty comes from the fact that the early Church of the 2nd and 3rd centuries was influenced, in its interpretation of baptism and the Eucharist, by the so-called mystery cults. These were religious rituals which originated from the East and experienced great resonance in the cosmopolitan Roman Empire. Through participation in what happened in these rituals people felt that they had, as it were, a connection with a divinity. That was often a divinity which promised the believers immortality, like Mithras, Isis or the Great Mother. We are familiar with the same phenomenon in the Macumba cult in Brazil or in the voodoo rituals in Haiti. In those days, for participation in the mystery cult it was necessary to be initiated. This required a long probation period, and the initiated, the so-called mystes, had to observe strict secrecy about what happened in the cult. The Greek root *my-* also means close (your mouth). The influence of the mystery cults is revealed, amongst other things, in the fact that baptism and the Eucharist are called in Greek *mysteria* (Greek was the language of the church also in Rome until the 3rd century); also in the fact that the Eucharist could only be given to the baptized (baptism was therefore a sacrament of initiation); and that the participants were not allowed to reveal, even to the catechumens, what took place there. A later relic of the influence of the mystery cults is expressions like "Easter mysteries", the "mysteries of the rosary", or the proclamation after the consecration: "Mystery of Faith". In these expressions we can be sure that believers interpret the word mystery as "mysteriousness, incomprehensibility" – and therefore completely misunderstand it. Mystery or secret mean in this context an event that takes place on two levels at the same time: on the visible level and on the deeper, spiritual level which is the level of reality.

When the preachers of the faith came from the south over the Alps to convert the Germanic peoples they brought these notions with them. But to operate on two levels at once was clearly a difficult task for the Germanic peoples. Efficacy suited them better. A sacrament became for them a holy intervention by God. Through a church ritual God himself would be involved, would intervene from out of his world in our world and produce something salutary: he would justify, bless, sanctify, forgive sins, decree deserved punishments, give eternal life, infuse "grace". All of that would happen when, for example, the priest pours a handful of water over the head of a new-born child and at the same time speaks the right words. All the effects are, by their very nature, invisible since they belong not to our world but to God's world. What was in the beginning a creative symbol of renewal and could be experienced as such at the baptism of an adult was reduced to a signal to heaven that it was to intervene. In reality the sacrament was in this way changed into a magic ritual.

This was not without consequences for the Eucharist. The early church was still clearly capable of consciously experiencing that "eating of the bread" was one and the same thing as existentially taking into oneself the glorified Jesus. Therefore the eternal life in John 6:26-51a could be called equally the fruit of active faith in Jesus and in 51b-56 the fruit of communion – repugnantly formulated there as eating Jesus' body and drinking his blood. What was possible for the early church is unfortunately no longer possible for us. We can still, indeed, intellectually grasp and accept the unity of communion and encounter with the glorified Jesus and therefore the unity of symbol and existential reality, but as children of a technological age we are no longer able to experience these two in their unity.

Review

Traditional teaching emphasizes very strongly that the sacraments are what fundamentally characterize our Catholic faith. But in fact they are less important than people think. They belong to the domain of ritual signs. And signs are not themselves what is existential and vital. They just draw attention to these. Moreover, signs always point to something else, and sacramental signs point to a deeper or higher reality. Unfortunately, with the sacraments we can hardly speak of them as signs any longer. In most cases they have been reduced to rituals which are, above all, sociologically important, i.e. for forming and identifying the Catholic group. And it is already good if they are not unconsciously understood as magical interventions. For with regard to baptism, the Eucharist, anointing of the sick, what remains of the original symbolic force of the bath, the shared meal, the anointing? Even where a sacramental rite still has an undiminished religious content and has not yet drifted away into magic, because of the impoverishment of its value as sign the sacrament will be experienced much less as a symbolic action than as a signal that is to set the other world in motion.

If we are to experience the sacraments as genuine and therefore creative signs of the divine we should no longer divide reality into two worlds. Only when the cosmos and man are seen as the visibility of the incomprehensible fundamental divine reality can human actions be seen as revelations of the creative activity of God. And this view of things is largely missing. The explanation of the supposed importance of the sacraments depends largely on the still dominant pre-modern views of our faith. But in modernity believers have put paid to such views.

They cannot accept the idea of an intervention from another world in answer to a signal or petition coming from our world. For modernity sacraments are now only important and healing as *mysteria*, i.e. as symbolic actions which, through the evocative creative power of the symbol, link the person with the richness of ultimate reality. But precisely in modernity such sensitivity to symbols has become, because of the pure objectivity of our thinking, an extremely rare thing.

Let us finish with a conclusion which has special significance for the Eucharist. With a certain amount of good-will, remembrance of Jesus' farewell supper could be called a source and a highlight of Christian life. The next chapter will deal with this. But this good-will ceases where the remembrance takes the form of a "Mass". Purely conceptually the Eucharist and the Mass are the same, but words have a content of feeling which is always present when they are used and which changes the content. "Mass" conjures up a whole which is comprised of strictly laid down ritual actions which come from the past. They are an amalgam of gestures and prayers without logical structure and context and they are permeated by a theology of sacrifice which modern man can only reject. The Tridentine Mass which Rome discreetly but clearly champions incorporates the idea of "Mass" still more clearly than Paul VI's more modernized form. Our gatherings of the faithful can be Eucharistic celebrations but they should cease to be Masses, however solemn a form these might be given.

For the faithful the Sunday service usually results in the satisfying feeling that the Sunday obligation has again been fulfilled. But what should the result have been? More social welfare work, a greater concern for good relationships at home, in the neighbourhood, in the area, in the community; more compassion with the disadvantaged people of the third and fourth world, more commitment to the preservation of creation. And as a source of inspiration for this work there should be more quiet, inwardness and prayer as a counterbalance to the superficiality with which we are flooded today by electronic entertainment. To want to exalt "Holy Mass" as a source and highlight of our lives as Christians shows a pious lacking in a sense of reality.

Chapter Six

Remembrance of the Last Supper

After the previous chapter it might seem that nothing much was left of what the Second Vatican Council calls the source and highlight of a fully Christian life and which in elevated language is called the "Eucharist" and in more ordinary language the "Mass". The difference between the two concepts is seen, amongst other things, in the fact that "Mass" can without any problem be used in the plural and can be made into an object of verbs like to order and to pay for. That betrays a significant materialization which is in stark contrast to the glorifying language of Church documents. Did anyone hear of ordering and paying for Eucharists? This criticism is therefore consciously levelled only at the Mass.

The glorifying language of the Council perhaps to some extent fits the original form of what the Mass became later on in the Middle Ages: the *synaxis*, literally: the coming together, in which the believers reflected on what Jesus had said and done at the Last Supper on the evening before his death. Did Jesus really want the twelve apostles later to keep on repeating this in memory of him? The tradition on which this story of the meal as told by Mark and Matthew depends shows no evidence of such a duty. This is only to be found in Paul and in Luke who is influenced by him. Clearly it spontaneously became in the Pauline churches a continually renewed remembrance and thus a liturgical custom.

This remembrance developed, as a result of an aberration, into an objective and practicable Mass. One aspect of this aberration was the interpretation of the Mass as a sacrifice through which something could be had from God: for example, an acquittal. There were also other possible favours, as when the cult of souls in purgatory reached its zenith in the Middle Ages, especially with the liberation of the "poor souls". Furthermore, there was also the unconscious conviction that a multiplicity of Masses was of proportionally great benefit to the Kingdom of God and the salvation of the world. And finally, without frequent participation in that ritual a way of life cannot be called fully Christian.

These very contestable views were the result of a pre-modern way of thinking which had no difficulty with the idea that when the Mass ritual is faithfully executed the other world propitiously intervenes – not automatically, of course, but no less surely. In this chapter there will be a detailed examination of the question about what the true value and place of the Mass in the life of the modern believer can be, since he has parted company with those mediaeval notions and has shaken off the whole supernatural fuss connected with the liturgy of the Mass. The encounter with Jesus who is living in glory as the saviour and as the revelation of God remains important for the believer's life. Perhaps a modern "this-worldly" treatment can open our eyes to the value of the original *synaxis* which has shrunk to become the Mass – a value which, through the fault of its mediaeval disguise, now escapes us. To this end only notions and expressions will be used which do not presuppose a supernatural world.

Speaking of the "sacrifice of the Mass" has become untenable

The shape of today's Mass is derived essentially from the Council of Trent. The product of more than 1000 years of development was purified of a multitude of accretions and fixed for the future. This is the form which Benedict XVI, after a modest amount of modernization by the Second Vatican Council, was trying to restore to its former dignity. It is characterized by a very strong accentuation of the sacrificial character of the Mass. This emphasis was not to be missing from the more modern form promulgated by Pope Paul VI after the Council. Rome insists that the Eucharist be seen as a sacrifice and indeed as a cultic sacrifice in the strict sense. A sacrifice is cultic when one deprives oneself of something valuable to give it to God by killing it, burning it, pouring it out or destroying it in some other way, in the belief that the divinity takes pleasure in such destruction. For Rome any interpretation of the Eucharist that ignores the sacrificial character is repugnant. This conception, of course, finds expression in the language of the prayers of the Mass and especially in the official Eucharistic prayers, which are totally permeated by notions of sacrifice.

And so the Mass is to be a cultic sacrifice. But then how does this relate to the sacrifice of the cross? For the Council of Trent there was not the slightest doubt that the death of Jesus on the cross was a true cultic sacrifice. It could fall back on the whole tradition, from Paul to the Fathers of the Church and the theologians right down to the declarations of official Church teaching. There was also no question that this sacrifice of the cross was of infinite value and thereby had made all further cultic sacrifices superfluous. This is confirmed in the letter to the Hebrews chapter 9. How then can the Mass be called a cultic sacrifice? The solution found by the Council of Trent was that the sacrifice of the Mass is to be seen as a *representatio* of the sacrifice on the cross. But this solution is a cul-de-sac, for the Mass is then almost like a stage presentation of Jesus' death on the cross, in which case it is no longer a real cultic sacrifice. Or this historical death on the cross is lifted out of its own historical period and made present in a later time, but now without the spilling of blood. But this is impossible. What is historical is essentially bound to time, is unique, and cannot be loosed from its historical context and transported into another time. Only *mythical* events can repeatedly be made present – precisely because they are mythical and not historical. There were, indeed, early attempts to interpret the Eucharist using concepts from the successful mystery cults. But these cults were completely mythical, so that, for example, in the Isis cult the mythical death and resurrection of Osiris could be experienced as an event in the present. But also when the celebrant on Holy Thursday solemnly says in the institution narrative: "On the day before his suffering and death, which is today", while it sounds sublime and impressive, it is mythical thinking. That evening which preceded the suffering and death of Jesus is, in reality, not today but an evening nearly 2000 years ago.

Every cultic sacrifice, including the sacrifice of the cross and the sacrifice of the Mass, presupposes a dubious conception of God, an image of an almighty power which demands satisfaction for faults committed but can be bought because it is prepared to engage in trading in the form of *do-ut-des*. And things become worse when the price God demands for this satisfaction is a cruel human sacrifice: namely, nothing less than the death of Jesus on the cross. This image of God contradicts Jesus' own image of God which he expresses in the word "Abba" and which provides the background for the parable of the Prodigal Son or the Lost Sheep.

Paul and the author of the Letter to the Hebrews did interpret the death of Jesus as a cultic sacrifice. But the meaningfulness of cultic sacrifice was to them as Jews of their time, as well as to their readers, totally unquestioned. With the aid of this theology of sacrifice they succeeded in removing to some extent the absurdity and scandal of Jesus' death on the cross which seemed completely to contradict his dignity as Messiah. But what was possible in the biblical mind-set of those days, where slaughter of sacrificial victims and expiatory sacrifices were established notions, is now no longer possible. Furthermore, the idea of cultic sacrifice is not compatible with a modern conception of God. Talk about the sacrifice of the cross and therefore also of the sacrifice of the Mass, no matter how established it may be, is nonsense for a modern believer.

As a link between the death of Jesus on the cross interpreted as sacrifice and the Mass which was likewise interpreted as sacrifice, the Council of Trent turned the Last Supper into a cultic sacrifice. "Jesus wanted to leave his church a visible sacrifice in which his sacrifice on the cross performed in blood would be represented in an un-bloody form (...), and he sacrificed his body and blood under the species of bread and wine; and with the words "do this in memory of me" he commanded his apostles, whom he instituted as priests of the new covenant, and their successors in the office of priesthood, to offer this sacrifice." Such a text reveals the abyss which opens up between the mediaeval thinking of the Counter Reformation and the thinking of modern believers.

But nowhere in the stories of the Last Supper is there any mention of Jesus offering himself as a sacrifice to the Father. This interpretation of the Eucharist seems to have emerged only in the 3rd century. In the cultural climate of the time, permeated with religion, the church needed to establish its own identity as a religion. To this end it had to be able to give evidence of sacrifices. But these had never existed in the church. The church was a community of believers expecting salvation exclusively from its bond with the glorified Jesus. It was not a religion with all the things that were typical of religions, such as sacrifices and priests. And so, for want of something better, they began to present the Eucharist as a sacrifice. The words which Jesus is supposed to have spoken as he passed around the cup and which included mention of a new covenant in his blood made this a possibility. Behind this we find the sacrifice of a bull at the conclusion of the (first) covenant (Exodus 24:5 and 8). As the idea of sacrifice penetrates into the Eucharistic gatherings the gradual transformation of the leader of the liturgy into a priest begins to take place, for priests are needed for sacrificial rituals. And with this transition, clericalization made its grand entry into the Church.

Even because of the pure heteronomy of the cultic sacrifice a modern believer has to baulk at an expression like "sacrifice of the Mass". Mass is an English translation of *missa* from popular Latin and originally meant sending away, dismissal. Because of the solemn final blessing after the Eucharistic gathering it gradually began to mean "dismissal with a blessing". In the 6th century it became the custom to give the name *missa* to the Eucharistic gathering itself, a meaningless name which says nothing about what the gathering was for. What should the event be named which recalls Jesus' last meal with his circle of followers on the evening before his death? Instead of Mass there are three other words to consider, all of them much older: the breaking of bread, the *synaxis*, the Eucharist.

A better name?

The first of the three, the breaking of bread, has the advantage of being purely inner-worldly without any supernatural overtones. Breaking bread is a Jewish synonym for "eating", comparable to the French expression *casser la croûte*. And the expression is to be found in the Acts of the Apostles 2:42 and 46. But here does it mean anything more than simply: eating with one another? In 2:46 the literal translation is: "Breaking bread in the different houses they shared a meal." But even if the expression here were to have referred to the Eucharist the following problems remain. First, breaking bread says just as little as *casser la croute* about the deeper meaning of this rite. Second, the expression by no means corresponds to what happens in our Masses, especially when *casser la croute* is in the back of our minds. Not only is no bread anywhere in evidence but only a thin wafer or "host" (literally, "sacrificial animal"), and also nothing is broken, apart from this one wafer, and this is not shared with the others present even though this is part of "breaking the bread". In short, this designation is making light of what really happens in the Mass.

A second, equally old name is *synaxis*, literally a gathering. While this word is not to be found in Sacred Scripture, the fact that the word is very old is clear from the fact that it is Greek. It originates from the 2nd or early 3rd century, for only in the 3rd century was Greek gradually superseded by Latin as the language of the Western Church. What speaks in favour of this name is that it is inner-worldly, but still more important that it contains an aspect of celebration which is more important than the rite itself: namely, the formation of a community. This aspect is stressed in the letter to the Romans 12:5: namely, as Christians we form one body, or in 1 Corinthians 10:17 where the role of the Eucharist is stressed as creating unity. The oldest description of what was later to become the Mass, a text from Justin around the year 150, begins with the mention of the gathering: "On Sunday all gather to share a celebration." The name *synaxis* highlights precisely this important aspect which is often missing in today's Mass.

There is also the fact that faith is essentially a community thing. We come to faith only through our fellow men. Just as we exist, grow and become what we are only through the society which supports us, we need this coming together for confirmation and strengthening of our faith. We experience this confirmation by praying and singing together, publicly proclaiming our faith and eating bread. The unity that already exists will be made visible in these many ways and will thereby be strengthened. Is there anything missing in the term *synaxis*? Yes. There is no reference to the content of this being together. Every prayer service is a gathering and strengthens the unity, but the Last Supper is not commemorated in every prayer service.

A third name is the current one, "Eucharist", literally: thanksgiving. This is giving thanks before eating. This name, too, is Greek and therefore likewise has its origins in the early church. It is already found in the *Didachè*, which is a believers' manual probably from as far back as the 1st century. In it we read: "With regard to the *eucharistia*, you should give thanks." Then follows the blessing of the cup and only then the blessing of the bread, and only the baptized are allowed to partake of the cup and the bread. But perhaps here we are dealing with a prayer of thanks at an *agapé*, the meal of friendship. In any case, giving thanks is something of this world, and that is already a first recommendation of this name. A second point is that it also teaches us something about the content of what then happens: we are concerned with a meal for which one gives thanks. Around the year 150 Justin describes the original form of today's Mass with the words: "The leader speaks prayers, as well as he can,– including prayers of thanks – over bread and wine. After the *Amen* spoken by the people, that for which thanks are given is shared by all." This mention of the people and the words "by all" points to the role played by the community in the event. But this name has the same weakness as the name *synaxis*: not every prayer of thanks before eating is a commemoration of what Jesus said and did at the Last Supper. And precisely this is the specific thing which the three names circle around without naming it. The fourth and best designation must therefore be: Remembrance of Jesus' Last Supper.

Remembrance of the Last Supper

Each of the two halves of this designation requires separate treatment. First, the concept of remembrance. This concept also fulfils the fundamental condition of belonging to this world, for it has nothing supernatural about it. It names a psychological return to the past, a thinking back – but to something important, something which addresses, fulfils, moves us deep within ourselves, and therefore not merely a good meal or a good excursion. It is a thinking back to something specially moving: for example, the death of a beloved person, a peace settlement, or the fall of the Berlin Wall. A remembrance is therefore also more than a purely rational process. It touches greater depths in us, we experience again a gripping event, not mythically, of course, but psychologically. And this presupposes that this event has moved us emotionally and can move us emotionally again. This points to the fact that we find something valuable in it, something good, and that we can encounter the transcendent in it. An encounter is always to some extent the forming of a union. In this sense we can affirm the words of John 6:40: "that all who see the Son (and this seeing should be understood as remembrance, since the text is directed to readers and listeners of the year 100 who had never seen Jesus) and believe in him (like the etymologically related praise, belief includes admiration and therefore a beginning of union) have eternal life (therefore fullness of life which is lasting and which can defy death)".

The fact that the Last Supper is written with initial capital letters indicates that not merely Jesus' last meal is meant but an important event which took place during this meal. In the three synoptic gospels and in 1 Corinthians 11:23-25 this event is narrated simply and with only slight variations. The significant aspect was not the action of breaking and distributing the bread, for that was usual for the head of the family or the host, but the interpretation Jesus gave to this action: namely, that he interpreted it as symbolically breaking and distributing himself. The same applies to the passing around of the cup. This is also not the significant point, although the use of the one cup was not the usual practice: normally each person drank out of his own cup. Here again the interpretation is remarkable: Jesus interprets the wine as his blood, but his meaning is that it is the symbol of his blood and therefore of his life force. The association of drinking and blood had to meet with strong inner resistance with authentic Jews, for in the Torah drinking blood is punished with death. But the reality of the wine overlaying the idea of drinking blood softens to some extent the spontaneous uncomfortable feeling.

What Jesus expresses in this way with a twofold sign is not easy to reduce to one formula. At any rate, it points to his desire that his disciples take him completely into themselves, merge with him, assimilate him. When the author of the fourth gospel replaces this narration with the washing of feet he shows that he understands this assimilation as sharing in Jesus' attitude of service. The participants in the rite should themselves be there for others.

Jesus' symbolic gift of self must have caught on with the witnesses, if not immediately (they probably did not yet understand what was happening before their eyes), then at least later when they began to reflect on its meaning. The written account in the gospel of how they were moved (for in all its simplicity the narrative is anything but a sober communication or an objective report) enables us to share in their emotion and thereby to be moved ourselves as if we were witnesses.

To think back to Jesus' gift of self and to be moved by it in such a way that our dedication to him is strengthened is also possible, of course, by non-ritual means: by prayer, contemplation, meditative reading. But to do it by means of the Eucharistic rite with bread and wine, and therefore by eating (and drinking) as at the Last Supper itself, has great advantages. First, it is a shared event just as the Last Supper was, and a person who joins with the believing community in which Jesus continues to live thereby joins himself more intimately with him. The biblical images of body and members and of the grapevine and the grapes occur in the New Testament precisely in a Eucharistic context. In 1 Corinthians 10:16-17 Paul says: "Because the (Eucharistic) bread is one, all of us form the one body", and the image of the grapevine and the grapes is found in John in the speech after the Last Supper.

The ritual remembrance with bread and wine has a further advantage over the inward and individual remembrance. A ritual is something tangible, material, and what is material has the capacity to serve as a symbol and thereby to open up the spiritual depths of reality. That presupposes that everything is genuine, for only what is genuine is also genuine as a symbol. That means that genuine bread should be used, not a paper-thin wafer. And the participants should also drink the wine that is understood as a symbol. That this works can be seen from the example of a large parish in Vienna. Here they put large dishes with pieces of bread and a jug of wine on the altar. For each participant who wants it a small earthen cup is filled from the jug. Only this eating and drinking makes the symbolical assimilation with the glorified Jesus real. Mere watching and praying piously are only surrogates. The broken and distributed bread, showing us the way Jesus is present in the world, loses much of its meaning if it is made into a pure object of adoration. The encounter with him is then limited to a meditative remembrance. But the imperative words of Jesus summon us to eat and drink. The awareness that Jesus wanted to be eaten and drunk loses its force. This means that forms of piety like Corpus Christi processions and "Eternal Adoration" are problematic, no matter how highly prized and faithfully practised by the pre-modern churchgoers.

We can now see that "celebratory remembrance of the Last Supper" is the best name suggested so far. Not only is remembrance something within this world (the object is an historical event) that brings no supernatural interventions from God-in-Heaven, but it also shows the content which brings the believers together: not a sacrifice but a ritual remembrance of Jesus' farewell action. We can honestly say of this remembrance something that cannot be said of the ordered and paid for Mass (especially where, in most of these cases, it concerns purgatory): that it is the source of all Christian life. Commemorating with bread and wine what Jesus revealed at his farewell meal as his attitude of serving and his gift of self can only have the effect of encouraging a similar attitude in us. Affirming this fundamental attitude in Jesus, which is what we are in fact doing in this commemoration, can rightly be called a highlight of Christian life. For here we are given a share – a beginner's share, at least – in the self-giving of Jesus even though in a ritual and therefore only symbolic form. But afterwards, and inspired by this celebration we will share in it in the real form of commitment to fellow men. And what is more deserving of the name "highlight" of our Christian life?

This self-gift of Jesus is more in evidence with the Last Supper than with the cross. The cross only shows what others did to him and the horrible things he had to endure. But that this cruel death meant a gift of self is not immediately clear. By contrast, his actions and his interpretation of them when he breaks bread and passes around the cup make it abundantly clear that he is giving himself to his fellow men.

In commemoration of this action, we encounter this self-giving Jesus in reality, for commemoration produces presence. And we encounter him there most really when we take up his offer, when we eat and drink what he offers us: namely, himself in the symbols of bread and wine. But if we experience bread and wine here (only) as symbols and therefore the presence of the glorified Jesus (only) as a symbolical presence, we are in direct collision with two of the traditional articles of faith specially pronounce at the Council of Trent: first, that bread and wine are essentially changed into the body and blood of Jesus – which is referred to by the mediaeval technical and almost unutterable term *transubstantiation* – and, second, that it is thereby no longer a question of a symbolical but a real, almost material presence of Jesus.

Change of essence and real presence

With change of essence, or transubstantiation, the church emphasizes since the Council of Trent that the celebrant's words of consecration bring about a substantial change of the bread and wine. The bread is no longer bread, it now only looks like bread, but in reality it has become the body of Jesus. The same applies to the wine, which has been changed into blood. To prevent misunderstandings, tradition adds that the "body of Jesus" refers to the whole person Jesus as he was seen and touched by his disciples after his resurrection, i.e. with flesh, bones, skin, hair, spirit and divinity. "Blood" also does not refer only to the fluid in his veins but to him in his entirety – not by virtue of the words of consecration but *per concomitantiam*, concomitantly. For just as it is not possible to have a living body without blood there is no living blood without a body. There is no need to be an unbeliever to be left speechless at this point.

The second element strongly accentuated by tradition follows from the first. It is the so-called real presence of the resurrected Jesus of Nazareth. The only reality that is there after the consecration is the risen person himself. Bread and wine are then only illusions. To cut off any escape route, the Council of Trent added after the words "genuinely and really present" the third defining concept "substantially present". From the context it is obvious what this concept was meant to make clear: that this presence of the risen one is a material presence, a presence in flesh and blood, skin and hair. For without that "substantially present" one might think that believing in a symbolic presence was enough, since also a symbolic presence, a presence in signs and images, is a real presence. Otherwise there would be simply no presence. No, says the Council, to believe in a purely symbolic presence is not enough. Anyone daring to do this *anathema sit*, should be expelled (from the community of believers).

Not only modern unbelievers but also modern believers are struck dumb by this language. The change of bread into a human body not only without any *noticeable* change but through the mere speaking of a short sentence belongs to the realm of fable or magic. The church's answer that it is not the seemingly magical power of the words that accounts for the change but the intervention of God-in-Heaven and that this intervention comes infallibly when a man (not a woman!) empowered through hierarchical channels pronounces the right words is supremely heteronomous thinking. What is also strange in this is that the veneration of the bread consecrated in this way has been inseparably bound up with the white wafer, which one cannot honestly call bread. If the celebrant, at the words "Behold the lamb of God", instead of this wafer were to hold up a Turkish flatbread and display it (and this was the bread in fact used at the Last Supper) the pious people in the church would protest, full of annoyance: "But that is not the Lamb of God, that is a Turkish loaf of bread!" Only a wafer can be the Lamb of God, genuine bread cannot be.

The almost material essential change canonized by the Council of Trent is now inconceivable for the modern believer. As a man of flesh and blood Jesus had only one body, not several. Even for the most stolid defender of the traditional view it must surely be unthinkable that at the Last Supper Jesus held this one body under the form (or appearance) of bread in his own hands. And it is still more inconceivable that he multiplied this body, which was just as material and indivisible as our bodies, as many times as the number of pieces of (seeming) bread he passed around to his guests at table. The most astounding thing is that no one – neither pope nor bishop nor theologian nor any half-enlightened believer seems to have seen this obvious truth. And if even at the Last Supper the bread could not become his material body and the wine his material blood but remained bread and wine and became the symbol of his gift of self, how then could it be different at the commemoration of that supper?

But the force of a unanimous tradition stifled the emergence of this insight right down to the present day. And if anyone did come across this evidence and dared to formulate it, condemnation was not long in coming. If he did not recant his heresy, prison and worse awaited him. One of these condemned men was Berengarius of Tours in the 11th century. It seemed clear to him that the consecrated bread was still bread but was the body of Christ insofar as it had become a representation of his body. He had to make a public denial of this insight, which he did for his own safety. Basically, Berengarius said 1000 years ago what the modern believer who has given up a God-in-Heaven should be saying today. His understanding of the "real presence" should simply be different from that of the Council of Trent. At the same time he should then show that in the language of a modern view of the world he is saying exactly what tradition in its pre-modern language was saying. What follows is an attempt to do this.

Existential and symbolic presence

What then can we as modern believers take the "real presence" to mean? As has already been said, every presence is real, even a symbolic one, otherwise we are not talking about presence at all. Tradition itself is aware of this and later so is the *Catechism of the Catholic Church* (no. 1374), but the Church is afraid that justice will not be done to the genuineness of this presence. In this it loses sight of the fact that, what it calls "substantial" presence and then to all intents and purposes understands as a material presence, is really only a symbolical presence. For our body is essentially only the sign, the symbol of our person, not our person itself.

For a modern clarification which includes tradition it is necessary to distinguish between existential and symbolic presence. To this end we should take as our starting point a modern believer's interpretation of the resurrection of Jesus: namely, that Jesus "is alive". This is not descriptive language but it says that through his surrender in accepting death he has achieved complete union with the fundamental reality, God, and has thereby reached ultimate perfection. And because the cosmos is the self-expression of the fundamental reality, God fills the whole cosmos with his presence. In this sense the fully perfected Jesus is present in all things, and indeed in a real sense, existentially.

Normally we are not aware of this presence. But it can be lifted into our consciousness. This step changes his latent, hidden presence into an actual presence, and we can say that he is then symbolically present. Symbolically, because the encounter with him takes place with the aid of material things which then become transparent, reveal their inner depths and thereby become signs, symbols. Thus Jesus can appear in all kinds of shapes as we "see" him in all these things. We can think, for example, of the Easter Night fires, the Easter Candle, the crucifix, the altar, the baptismal water, an icon that represents him, a Bible text. When on Easter Night the praise of the Easter Candle is sung the object of this praise is not the three kilogrammes of beeswax. And at the veneration of the cross in the Good Friday liturgy it is not a piece of wood that is being honoured, but we are celebrating in song Jesus who lives forever. We can know him also in people. Veneration of saints is the implicit but also real awareness of his presence in people. He can also appear to us in the form of the needy because he has identified himself with them, as the judgement scene in Matthew 25:31-46 shows. It is true that the choice of words "to the least of my brethren" and the mention of those locked up in prison (at the time of Matthew this was a reality, but not yet in the time of Jesus) suggests that the author was thinking particularly of Christians in need.

Also at the Last Supper we are concerned with a form of symbolically real presence. Jesus could see himself in every piece of bread because he lived as if he were bread, completely there for his fellow men, devoted to them and nourishing them. That does not mean that he actually saw himself so. All things are self-revelations of – and therefore symbols of – the creative fundamental reality. But normally we do not see things in this way. Instead, we see them as useful or harmful, pleasant or unpleasant for us. It is only in privileged moments that we see them as symbolic manifestations of the fundamental mystery. Jesus' departure from his disciples (and from life) was certainly a very special, moving moment. On that evening he suddenly saw the bread on the table quite consciously as a representation of himself and saw himself quite consciously as this bread. This is precisely what he wanted for his disciples who were so very dependent on him. Soon they would be deprived of his presence. He wanted them to be permanently filled with his spirit, his vision, his inspiration; he wanted to enrich them with the best things he had himself. He did not *make* the bread on the table into a symbol of himself: he simply saw himself in this bread. That is exactly what he was. The potential symbolic value of this bread, the latent comparison between him and the bread becomes real for him in this moment. He did not bring about any wonderful change. He did not say that he was changing the bread into something else. He said what he saw: that in this bread he saw his body (a Semitism for person), his self, that this bread was as it were his self. He said that that bread was essentially different from the item of food that it outwardly was and remained. It was the perfect image of himself.

What remains of this when we commemorate what Jesus experienced and did in those moments? When we utter again the words in which he expressed what he saw and experienced in the bread, our eyes are opened to the symbolic value of the bread that is lying there. We see it as Jesus saw it. That was previously not yet the case. The bread was previously only bread, an item of food. But now we too see Jesus in this bread. His presence now becomes symbolically real. This shows how important it is that the bread on the table is really bread and that we can eat it. The knowledge of his presence will only become fully genuine when we eat of it, for bread only becomes genuine bread, i.e. life-giving nourishment, when it is eaten. This makes the prescribed use of the usual thin wafers very questionable. In blind loyalty to the Jewish tradition of the unleavened Passover bread the wafers continue to be used instead of genuine bread and have thereby become for the faithful the natural form of Eucharistic bread. But they do not merit the name of bread. And if, instead of these, genuine bread is used one should not sound the alarm and talk blusteringly about prohibitions but be grateful that the Eucharist is finding its way back to its real form.

To experience and affirm the symbolic presence of Jesus in the Eucharist naturally presupposes that he is important to us, that he plays a creative role in our lives, precisely as a person given to us as a gift. But likewise on Good Friday we cannot honestly venerate the crucified if he is not important to us precisely as the crucified. Otherwise the veneration of the cross becomes an empty ritual which does not influence our lives. In the same way, without a true bond with Jesus, belief in his presence in the symbol of the bread is reduced to an intellectual act which does not enrich us.

Thus it is not the words "This is my body" which make Jesus present, as the mediaeval church authorities have proclaimed in an unconscious kind of magical thinking. In the Council of Trent they said, namely, that the real presence came about *vi verborum*, by power of the words (spoken over the bread and wine) and they called on the authority of Matthew 26:26 where they read that the disciples only received the body of Jesus after he had spoken the words (which in the eyes of the Church authorities were the decisive ones). But in fact in the Greek text it is the other way round. At the words over the cup in Mark 14:23-24 this becomes still clearer: "They drank from the cup and Jesus said (afterwards) ..." And so at the Last Supper it was not the words spoken in an almost magical way which worked a miracle. The same must be true for the remembrance celebration of the meal. The bread that is shared (if this can be said of the Communion, for it does not look like sharing) becomes the symbol of Jesus' self-communication. And this is what it becomes when thanks to the ritual, the core of which is the narration about Jesus' actions and the words accompanying these actions, we see in this bread the intense symbol of his very being, the image of his readiness to be as bread to his fellow men. The rite makes him symbolically – but really – present in our midst as delivering himself and nourishing us spiritually.

The way in which the Eucharist and therefore also the Last Supper was spoken of traditionally is no doubt simpler. Everyone immediately understands what happens in the so-called consecration according to the pre-modern conception: a man endowed with supernatural power and using a sacred formula changes bread into the body of Jesus and then wine into his blood. But changing bread into a human body and wine into human blood by using words which smack of magic is, from a modern point of view, pure wizardry and therefore unthinkable. And as a defence against criticism to call on the almighty power of God, for whom nothing is impossible, does not help, for the notion of a God-in-Heaven intervening and working miracles and being brought into action by the priest is for modern people no less inconceivable. All that remains then is the laborious attempt we have just made to make the tradition of the presence of God in the signs of bread and wine accessible for the modern believer.

Surprising consequences us. But that can happen also outside the liturgy, even

The essence of the Eucharist consists therefore in our doing what Jesus himself did at the Last Supper, namely, to see him in the bread for what he is: a person who out of human love is totally given to us out of human love and thereby nourishes privately.

With the bread on our table we can become aware that all bread, concretely also this bread, is symbolic of Jesus and makes him present, and while eating it we can gratefully be aware of his symbolically real presence. This happens better, of course, in a community of believers in which the others also experience the same thing. Besides, a fixed ritual is desirable, since a community's prayer requires a certain order, otherwise there is a danger of chaos. In 1 Corinthians 14:26-40 Paul draws attention to this danger. Ritual helps furthermore to transcend the objective dimension in which bread is only an item of food. One of the functions of the ritual action consists precisely in opening for us a deeper dimension than that of the everyday and thereby giving us access to the transcendent.

Of course, to achieve such awareness and to have such an experience of the presence of Jesus a specially consecrated magician is not needed. The theology of sacrifice and the Tridentine doctrine of the change of essence have no role to play in this, and there is no longer anything left of the supposed value of the official Mass any more than there is of the earlier obligation to take part in this traditional ritual on Sundays. The only obligation that remains is to grow in faith and in love through the encounter with the living Jesus. For this encounter, experienced in the remembrance of his self-surrender, the best place is undoubtedly the community of those who cherish the same belief in Jesus as our saviour and, like us, know him through the symbol of bread. But if we do not find a community whose way of celebrating the Eucharist helps us in this, there is still the possibility of celebrating this remembrance in the way described above. That will bind us more to Jesus than an unsatisfying Mass ritual. And it is precisely this bond that we should always be concerned with.

But where there *is* a question of a symbolic presence there is nothing to be said against it. It is even good if this is also made clear in the so-called institution narrative, for example by the celebrant saying: "Take and eat of this bread, which is like my body." But where the ritual celebration in a community of modern believers has taken on a contemporary form, the participants should never lose sight of the fact that to eat with one another without becoming aware of the symbolic depth of what one is doing is not a remembrance of the Last Supper.

And what if after the meal some bread is left over? For Calvin it has then become ordinary bread again. But if one wants to manage the symbolic value of what one has experienced – and that is a psychological attitude as is faith as well – keeping it with reverence has some meaning. But this meaning requires that one eat this bread as a believer and not keep it permanently in order to adore it and carry it around in a procession.

What for the modern believer is the awareness of the presence of Jesus in the bread symbol, for the pre-modern believer takes the form of belief in his bodily presence. It is important to realize what a string of heteronomous views one has to subscribe to in this: that Jesus is at the same time both man and God; that therefore for him nothing is impossible; that he physically rose from the dead and still consists of flesh and blood and also of bones and skin and hair, although immaterially, spiritually according to Paul in 1 Corinthians 15 – but how are we to conceive of this? –; that through the words "Do this in memory of me" he gave the eleven or twelve apostles the duty and the power, with a very definite set of words, to bring about this bodily ("substantial") presence, that at the same time he empowered these eleven or twelve to pass on this power selectively (namely, only to men), that reality and its appearance can be completely separated from one another. It would be possible to add to this list. But for a believer who has accepted modernity this is just too much.

Yet despite all differences, the pre-modern and the modern experience of the Eucharist are in agreement about what is essential: seeing Jesus in the sign of bread and wine and finding salvation through our turning to him which is expressed in eating the bread and drinking the wine. Both ways of looking at the Eucharist are in agreement that what is truly important is the growth in our existential turning to Jesus which takes place in our true encounter with him by means of the Eucharistic rite. Whether we speak then of an essential change and substantial presence or, better, of an encounter through symbols, is of secondary importance. The two ways of looking at it are saying the same thing with the aid of different thought categories. Ultimately the only important thing is our existential union with Jesus. The different ways of expressing it do accentuate different things. But both are agreed that communion without awareness and turning to him is only empty ritual. Paul himself sharply criticizes this in 1 Corinthians 10 by means of a comparison with the old Israel, and in 11:29 he rages vehemently against the false way in which the Corinthians celebrate "the Lord's Supper". Obviously for some of them the ritual was more important than existential union with the living Jesus Christ.

Chapter Seven

Atheism as the Final Step

This book began by recalling the words of Dietrich Bonhoeffer: "We should live in the world – *etsi Deus non daretur*. (...) We should live like people who manage life without God." The Latin phrase was quoted from memory. It refers back to words of the father of international law, Hugo Grotius: *etiamsi daremus Deum non esse*: "even if we were to accept that there is no God." For Bonhoeffer the meaning of Grotius's unfulfilled condition has changed. It fluctuates between: even if there were no God, and: as if there were no God.

With this interpretation of the sentence Bonhoeffer has pointed out the direction which our ideas as believers and our lives as Christians should take if we want to be at home in the 21st century and bring a liberating message for our contemporaries. And liberation, in the church's language: redemption, is surely the *alpha* and *omega* of our faith as Christians. This book and the previous one, *Living in God without God*, are an attempt to develop this intuitive insight of Bonhoeffer. This concluding chapter aims at showing the ultimate consequences of this intuition. And these can cause confusion for many people, but unnecessarily so. For even if (or: although) there is no *theos*, no God-in-Heaven, everything that is essential to our faith as Christians is untouched. And this is also part of Bonhoeffer's fundamental intuition, as the following sentence from a second theological letter from prison proves: "When we are ultimately forced (...) to see Christianity as a porch at the entrance to complete irreligiousness, what is the resulting position for us and for the church? How do we speak about God without religion? (...) How do we speak in a "secular" way about God, how are we Christians in a way that is secular and without religion?" Without religion, therefore without God and therefore godless, a-theistic. And yet Christians. The Christian of the future is to be someone who thinks and acts a-theistically. Some people on hearing this will be shaken to the core. Others will protest in annoyance. Therefore we must look more closely at the concept of atheism.

For some years now the existence of God has been the subject of heated discussion. There is no end to the debates. But what are people speaking about? What is meant by the little word "God"? When we talk about a house everyone knows what is meant, no matter how many different kinds of house there may be. We see houses and we live in houses. But "God" is not a perceivable object. And yet people in all cultures of the past have been certain that they were dependent on invisible forces which they spontaneously imagined as persons and for the most part as similar to human beings. The reverential attitude of human groups with regard to these "gods" was expressed in rituals and confessions of faith. The totality of these rituals and confessions is called religion.

Religion seems to have emerged fairly late in the approximately one million years of the history of *homo sapiens*. No one knows when and how. But artefacts from cultures that go back 30,000 years or more seem to point to the presence of such ideas existing already in that time. In any case, such notions increasingly permeate all civilizations in the course of the further development of humanity, for always and everywhere man saw himself confronted with inexplicable and threatening natural phenomena against which he was defenceless. In his psyche they took on the form of invisible personal powers. They became gods, in Greek *theoi*, which people thought existed up above, probably because the specially destructive phenomena – for example, thunder and lightning, storms and hurricanes – came from on high. Man's attitude to these divine powers was similar to his attitude to the social powers which ruled society: he submitted to them, revered them, praised them, offered them gifts, i.e. made sacrificial offerings, and tried in this way to get something from them. Religion was born, and every civilization developed its own forms of religion. And because the Greek *poly-* means "many" the first form of religion which was disseminated everywhere was called polytheism.

That remained so for many thousands of years. But about 3,000 years ago in the Near East a form of religion sprang up amongst people in later Palestine, the Jews. In this religion only one God was known. Because the Greek root *mono-* means "sole, only" this new form is called monotheism. Up to this point God was a generic name which could be used as a predicate for all kinds of supernatural and therefore invisible powers. But in the future the word could be used as a proper noun in the singular and could refer to a unique power which rules everything. Out of Judaism emerged 2,000 years ago a particular form of monotheism which underwent an astonishing development. It would become the basis for our reckoning of time, and around the year 1000 Christianity would be the only form of religion in the West.

But in the 19th century the West experienced the birth of yet another new religious phenomenon. The Jewish-Christian image of God which had cleared away all the earlier images of God suffered the same fate in its own territory. Just like Baal, Zeus, Jupiter or Wotan, in the Christian West the Christian *theos* was dismissed as an illusion. Western culture is becoming increasingly a-theistic. "A-theistic" is of itself synonymous with "god-less". It is just that "atheistic" in contrast to godless has become to some extent acceptable. In the US, however, atheist is just as negative as godless. Anyone seeking public office there should not admit to the voters that he is an atheist. His chances of being elected would immediately be cut in half. And condemnation of atheism is much greater outside the Western world than it is in the US. A black African is amazed if he hears it said that there is no God. To his ears this is absolutely crazy. And a Muslim explodes with anger at the denial of the existence of Allah. Also in the West during the Middle Ages and up to the Enlightenment there would be no mercy for people who denied the existence of God. This shows how exclusively atheism belongs to the modern European view of life and that it must be closely associated with the Enlightenment. The atheistic West is (for the time being) a lonely island in an ocean of religions.

But the threat of inexplicable natural phenomena is only one of the two roots of religion. That fear produced the gods, an idea of the ancient Greek thinker Epicurus which is again finding resonance in the West, is not a sufficient explanation. Innate in man there must be a sense that he belongs to a greater reality which therefore transcends him. Otherwise he would never have elevated those powers to the status of gods. We can see theism as an expression of this sense and monotheism as an improved version of it, characterized by the view that above the universe thrones a single personal power thought to be male. It rules freely over man and the cosmos and lays claim to veneration and obedience. The atheist denies that there is such a *theos* even though in doing so he has to defy prevailing opinions. It is, namely, clear to him that such a being makes free human beings into slaves. He recognizes himself in the mythical Prometheus who dares to challenge the gods by stealing fire from them for the benefit of man, knowing that he will incur frightful punishment for his act. For the atheist Karl Marx, Prometheus is the most important saint and martyr in the philosophical calendar.

But denial of the existence of a *theos* does not yet mean denial of the sense just referred to in man and therefore denial of transcendence. Many atheists act according to values which they consider more important than their own little egos. They experience these values as superior to their ego and therefore as transcendent. A sentence from Albert Einstein is an excellent illustration of this. "Sensing that behind all that we can experience something is hidden which our intellect is not able to grasp, something the beauty and sublimity of which come to us only indirectly and like a pale reflection, is religion. In this respect I am a deeply religious atheist." Genuine denial of the divine is only to be found in a materialism which sees the self as the highest value and in this way in fact denies transcendence. This attitude is well illustrated by the words attributed to the French king Louis XV: "Après moi le déluge!", after me the deluge. In other words, as long as it does not affect me it does not matter what happens.

Atheism as a phase in evolution

As we have said, it is only since the Enlightenment that one can speak of atheism as a farewell to religion and therefore to the collective acknowledgement of and reverence for a *theos*. Thus atheism is essentially a modern phenomenon and belongs to the monotheistic Christian West. When the Roman poet Lucretius in his *De rerum natura* vehemently attacks religion this is not atheism in the modern sense, since for him as an Epicurean there is still the world of the gods. But between these and men there is no relationship. Modern atheism presupposes therefore passing beyond the polytheistic stage of human history.

This development required millennia. It begins with the transition from primitive polytheism to so-called henotheism (the Greek root *hen-* is the number one) in which the original unordered multiplicity of the gods took on the form of a large family under a primordial father whom the other gods had to obey: Zeus for the Greeks, Jupiter for the Romans, Odin for the Germanic peoples. The transition from this henotheism to monotheism began around 1000 BC in the Near East with the politically and culturally quite insignificant people Israel. This culture was inwardly strong enough to practise its own ever more clearly pronounced monotheistic cult of Yahweh despite the polytheistic influences surrounding it in the Near Eastern cultural world. Monotheism is, in fact, a progressive step by comparison with polytheism. The ethical demands of Yahwism also clearly outstrip those of neighbouring peoples. The deeply humanistic quality of its views is revealed, for example, in the protest of the prophets in Israel against the oppression and exploitation of the weak. However, in Israel itself the transition from henotheism to monotheism was a laborious process which took several centuries and, as the two Books of Kings tell us, did not come about without bloodshed. The toughness with which a culture fights for its religious notions shows the importance it attaches to its link with the transcendent. Explosions of rage as after the burning of some pages of the Koran or after the publication of caricatures of the prophet Mohammed have provided a recent illustration of this.

The victory of Yahwism within Judaism was only finally achieved in the 6th century BC as a consequence of the exile of the Jewish people in Babylon. Under the influence of inspired preachers like Jeremiah and Ezekiel the deportees in Babylon affirmed their Jewish identity by distancing themselves from the polytheism of the surrounding environment, orienting them-selves exclusively on Yahweh. This means that around 500 BC Yahweh was the unique power which, for the Jews, had a claim to the title "God".

The victory of monotheism in an insignificant little people in the Near East was to have world-wide consequences. In the first five centuries after the Babylonian Exile there was as yet no trace of this. But then within Jewish Yahwism a mutation, as it were, occurred with the appearance of the prophetic figure of Jesus of Nazareth, and the mutated part developed into Christianity. For its part, this Christianity showed its spiritual superiority over the many Hellenistic cults in the midst of which it lived. It grew slowly but constantly, without fuss, propaganda, or the use of force – solely from its own inner strength – and became established as the most important cult form in the Roman Empire. Then, when the Emperor Constantine the Great saw in the church a precious ally and became her protector, she began to use her privileged position to oust other cult forms both by political and violent means. Later Charlemagne would deal with the heathen Saxons in the same unevangelical (because warlike) way. And still later the Spanish conquerors in Latin America would do the same with the Indians. In the long run the Christian form of monotheism became the only religion in Europe and America. In Asia and North Africa the same thing happened with Islam, another form of monotheism which emerged in Arabia but which was inspired by Christianity and Judaism. The name of the Jewish-Christian *theos* was changed to Allah. The upshot of this is that the monotheism born in the tiny space of Judaism is now the form of religion for half of humanity.

But in the 17th century the Dutch diplomat Hugo Grotius, in his seminal book about international law, *De jure belli et pacis* (about law in war and in peace), wrote a sentence of which no one, not even himself, realized the import: "Even if we were to suppose that there is no God natural law would not be affected." Unconsciously the pious Grotius had sown the seed of atheism. From this sentence it follows that there is something more absolute than God: namely, man's law, since natural law is man's law. But if there is anything more absolute than God then God is not the absolutely transcendent. And then human law is also not his creation because even without him there would be human law. And if human law is not his creation then neither is man his creation because that law belongs to man's nature. Without realizing it, the Christian believer, Grotius, undermined with this sentence the whole of Christian doctrine.

The seed he unknowingly sowed needed another two centuries to sprout and to burgeon. First the modern sciences had to reach such a level of development that would enable them to give a coherent inner-worldly explanation for all natural phenomena so that man would no longer need to have recourse to a *theos* which was outside the cosmos and therefore invisible and not demonstrable. The year 1750 can serve as the beginning of this process of enlightenment, the year in which Benjamin Franklin, at the risk of his life, provided proof that lightning was not an intervention of God-in-Heaven but a gigantic electrical discharge, a purely inner-worldly phenomenon. One and a half centuries later, in scientific circles there was hardly any more talk of divine interventions. Previously it had been thought that God was everywhere at work. Around 1900 he was seen to be nowhere at work. His existence was not denied, only forgotten. He played no part in the bustle of scientific activity. Everything ran smoothly without him. One of the consequences was that under the influence of science in the West, religion, cult, church were now of secondary importance. For a while they were not given up. The iceberg of the past only melts away slowly. Besides, human beings need rituals, and the church rituals are rich and beneficial. Thus Christianity, for better or for worse, could survive quite a long time in a culture which was steadily becoming less religious.

For the once all-powerful church, the situation was gradually becoming more dangerous than it realized. In more educated circles it was clearly losing ground. The Enlightenment ideas were continually gaining in influence and its devotees became more and more sharply critical of church teachings, which proved to be very susceptible to refutation. The Lisbon earthquake of 1755, with more than 30,000 deaths, gave rise to a question which after Auschwitz would resound a hundred times louder: where was the almighty and at the same time infinitely good God during this catastrophe? Was he anywhere at all? Did he still exist? Do not misery and evil in the world contradict the existence of a being which is at the same time almighty and infinitely good? For if he was not able to prevent such catastrophes he was not all-powerful, and if he was able and yet did not do it (and he clearly did not do it) he was not infinitely good. This 3rd century argument, wrongly attributed to Epicurus, returned during the Enlightenment with great force. Those who were still strongly religious took refuge in deism: God does exist, but after he superbly planned the universe and commanded that it exist, the *Grand Architecte de l'Univers* no longer concerned himself with events in this sublunary world. There was no point in asking him for anything, and also no point in adoring him, and the unloved institution, the Church, could be left aside. The great exodus from the Church now began.

One further step and the disappearance of God's effectiveness brought the denial of his reality, for if he no longer played a role in the cosmos and his existence even seemed contradictory what was the basis for saying that he exists? What began as doubt and questioning became, in the long run, denial. Modern atheism was born. The burden of proof of divine reality was now with the believers, therefore with the Church, for anyone who maintains something controvertible should be able to prove that he has good grounds for his assertion. But everything which earlier had served as proof of God's influence and therefore of his reality – thunder and lightning and apparitions and miracles and so one – could now clearly be explained by inner-worldly causes. Interventions by an almighty God were not at all necessary, not even for explanations of the order and purpose in living nature, from which Cicero had already concluded that an ingenious and perfect creator existed. The evolution theory of Darwin and de Vries provided a coherent inner-worldly explanation of this order and purpose: namely, natural selection of non-directed, therefore aimless but randomly favourable mutations occurring in the course of astronomically long periods of time. No gap remained in the scientific explanations, and the God from another world, the God of the Gaps, who earlier was deemed necessary to fill the gaps due to our ignorance, had served his purpose. To want to introduce him somewhere nevertheless, would be to cast doubt on the validity of scientific explanations and therefore on the reliability of human reason. Scientific laws are the genuine children of this reason and anyone who repudiates the children repudiates the mother. Then all thinking ceases, for without reliance on reason there can be no more scientific certainties and no more reliable thought.

Furthermore, the existence of a God who creates everything was completely contradictory to enlightened thinking. For this existence would mean the complete dependence of the cosmos. But such dependence would question the autonomy of the cosmos and its laws which modernity can no longer doubt. And how would it be possible to reconcile human freedom, which amounts to independence and is constitutive of the human being, with that dependence?

It is necessary to realize that modern atheism does not consist of blind assertions and vengeful enmity towards the church, although the latter has definitely played a role. It is committed to achieving important goals and is backed up by arguments. It is basically the battle of human reason and human freedom against their disempowerment by religious worldviews, within which one is only allowed to think logically further when one has blindly accepted some pre-existing views thought up by other people.

The high level of commitment explains the vigour of the duel between modern thinking and religion. If the Christian message is to be taken seriously in the modern era, atheism is not to be condemned but assimilated.

Gain and loss

To begin with, a balancing account in this new phase of human spiritual history is needed. First the loss statement. Friedrich Nietzsche, surely one of the luminaries of modern atheism, saw that the disappearance of religion had to end in catastrophe for a civilization which depended so fundamentally on its belief in a God-in-Heaven. In *Die fröhliche Wisssenschaft* he expressed his premonition of what was threatening after the "death of God" by putting his words into the mouth of a fool who in broad daylight rushed into the market-place with a lantern shouting that a dreadful disaster was about to befall Western culture. The "death of God" would bring down with it the whole of Western civilization with all its spiritual richness, its ethics, its creative art, its search for and discovery of truth. But that did not happen. Un-believing modernity concludes from this that Western civilization is not so indebted to Christianity as it seemed to be, and that the values of modern Europe are less the fruit of Christianity than of the humanism of the Enlightenment, which was itself, via the Renaissance, indebted to Greek and Roman antiquity.

As a corrective to this conclusion it is worth pointing out at least one form of humanizing which Europe, without the slightest doubt, owes to the church: namely, the mighty flood of care for people, especially for those who in all cultures are abandoned. These are people with contagious diseases, the insane, the orphans, needy elderly people, lepers, all kinds of disabled persons, and the homeless. The Roman Empire did not even have a word for hospital or orphanage because they did not know of such things. And none of the innumerable organizations in that empire had as its aim to support people in need. Care for the poor was simply unknown there. But "feeding the hungry, clothing the naked ..." from Matthew 25 was and still is a daily reality in the church. The Abbey of Cluny, for example, each year provided a meal for 18,000 people in need and these were fuller meals than were to be found on the plates of the monks. Care for the disabled began with initiatives taken by Christians, and still today care of the lepers in China, India and Africa is 95% work done by Christians. Clearly reverence for God which takes its inspiration from Jesus of Nazareth has in it a human potential not to be found in this measure outside of this community of believers. This inspiration puts out of commission the principle that one hand washes the other. It is concerned with selfless service. Of course, modern humanism can refer to the humanitarian commitment of Médecins sans frontières or Amnesty International. But medical missionary Sisters had been operating half a century before Médecins sans frontières saw the light of day. And where do you find in modern humanism a commitment to fellow men to compare with that of a Damian De Veuster, an Abbé Pierre, a Mother Teresa? In the meantime, Western society and therefore precisely that part of the world in which Christianity enriched culture for a thousand years, has taken over a large part of social care. And it should be so. But it has only taken on and developed, often – above all, technically and bureaucratically – what Christians had started and continue with unlimited generosity and perseverance and at the cost of innumerable sacrifices. The reality is that the modern helpers are often dwarves standing on the shoulders of giants.

Humanistic ethics and its limits

It had been Nietzsche's great fear that with the death of God the gigantic wealth of Western culture would sink without trace. That this catastrophe did not happen is something the West owes to another force which partly filled the vacuum which had resulted: namely, to atheistic modern humanism. The *theos*, God-in-Heaven disappeared, but the consciousness of a transcendent reality did not disappear with it. The *theos* was a transitional expression of it. Modern man rediscovered this transcendent reality in another form. The sacred aura which earlier surrounded the name "God" has now shifted to man. Man became untouchable, his rights became sacrosanct, everything should be done for his well-being and for his further human development. Religion made way for human service. In this soil a new ethics sprang up, a humanist one, the actual content of which was not very different from that of traditional church ethics. Many of its prescriptions correspond to the spirit of the gospel, some of them even more than those found in the Church's ethics. In Chapter Five we saw how piety in the church's past history could go hand in hand with appalling inhumanity and that very few voices were raised in opposition to it. In less than a century, modernity managed to eliminate some of these anti-human excesses. Believers had already opposed torture as a legal method of investigation or as a cruel form of execution, but only under the influence of enlightened thinkers like Montesquieu and Voltaire did it gradually become illegal in the last quarter of the 18th century, and in the Papal States only in 1815. The slave trade, which the very Catholic Portuguese and Spaniards had zealously practised for centuries, was outlawed in 1809, and slavery itself some decades later. Witch hunting, which, supported by theologians with arguments from the Bible, was rife since the end of the 15th century, and had brought thousands – mainly women – to the stake, disappeared gradually in the late 17th century under the influence of the emerging Enlightenment, which liberated people from belief in real devils. Only the Enlightenment had ended the dreadful deprivation of rights of which the Jews had been victims since the time of the crusades. And again it was this Enlightenment which put in the stocks of the world's conscience forced conversions, persecution of those who thought differently, intolerance, discrimination, and all other forms of denial of human rights which had been normal in the Christian *Ancien Régime*.

Anti-religious authors like Richard Dawkins or Sam Harris like to use the argument of evil that the religions have on their account. In this they are mainly concerned with Christianity and Islam. It is easy to cite a myriad of examples of such evil, from the crusades (and considerably earlier) through the wars of religion in Europe to Al-Qaida and "nine-eleven". Here the verdict is that of its very essence religion is a disaster for humanity. We should accordingly fight against it with all (legal) means. But something which, of its very essence, brings disaster and is not just a chance cause of disaster for humanity, must always and only produce disaster, and one has to be blind not to see that from the religions, and especially from Christianity, infinitely much that is good and precious has emerged and has wonderfully enriched humanity. Some examples have been cited above. The cause of evil in the religions must have a source which is different from religion itself.

Conversely, modern humanism, which boasts that it liberated humanity from the wicked witch called religion, produced exactly the same evil and often to a far greater degree than the church did previously: suppression, indoctrination, intolerance, persecution, inhumanity. In its quite short history a plethora of examples are to be found, from Nazism and Stalinism to Mao and Pol Pot. Obviously, both within religion and modern humanism another factor, lethal for true humanity, is at work and is spoiling both. This factor is the cold-blooded self-interest in the human heart, in the form of hunger for power, greed, contempt for mankind. Traditional Christianity spoke here of original sin from which we could be purified only by God-in-Heaven through Jesus Christ. We cannot redeem ourselves. By contrast, humanism maintains that our salvation is in our own hands. God-in-Heaven will not do it for us, for he does not exist. Once autonomous, always autonomous. Further on it will become clear that both positions are right. But to realize this, Christianity will have to give up God for God, i.e. give up the idea that a theistic view of God is an adequate reflection of the incomprehensible fundamental reality. It must arrive at the insight that its *theos* is, at the most, a finger which points to this unfathomable mystery which is gradually revealing itself in the course of evolution. For its part, atheism must give up the opinion that the church is only interested in this finger and not that to which it is pointing.

The care and commitment of both world views equally have humanization as their goal. The same unrelenting drive of the ultimate reality is revealed in both, for the self-expression of the fundamental reality, the evolving cosmos, drives both forward equally in this direction. If they were allies in this battle for liberation instead of opponents much would be gained for mankind. What Christians pray for in the Our Father, that the will of this fundamental reality be done, would be done. The kingdom, i.e. the rule of God would come about – will and rule, of course, understood as the language of imagery. And the opponents reconciled with one another would themselves gain from this: the advantage of one would be to the advantage of the other. And a great deal of creative energy would no longer be wasted on the wrangling in which humanity loses more than it gains. This reconciliation may seem inconceivable. Religion as belief in a *theos* and atheism as its denial seem to be like fire and water. Yet what here seems impossible is in fact possible. If of the many religions there is one that can integrate modern atheism it is Christianity. Atheism has sprouted in its soil. Precisely this is what Dietrich Bonhoeffer intuitively realized. What follows is an attempt to explain this.

Bonhoeffer and his religion-less Christianity

In the two great theological letters which he wrote in 1944 from the Nazi prison Spandau he advocates a Christianity that no longer looks up to a God-in-Heaven, a Christianity that is religion-less and in this sense is a-theistic. On 3 April he writes to his friend and later biographer Bethge: "How do we speak about God without religion (...), how are we Christians in a religion-less, secular way?" And on 16 July: "We must live as people who deal with life without God. (...) Before God and with God we live without God. The responsible world is more godless and therefore perhaps closer to God than the dependent world." This can give the impression of being a literary play with paradoxes which, looked at more closely, proves to be hollow and empty. But that is not at all the case. This will become clear when we go more deeply into his thought.

He uses the word "God" in two distinct ways. In "without God" and "godless" he is talking about the heteronomous, pre-modern notion of God, a God-in-Heaven, a *theos* which atheism has accounted for. In "living before God and with God" he is using the word in the sense of transcendence for which Paul Tillich, years before, had used the formulation "the depth of reality". Or in the sense of Einstein's words cited above about the sublime which is hidden behind all concrete experience. Bonhoeffer shows the stark contrast between the *theos* outside the cosmos and the God conceived of as inner-worldly, the Fundamental Love which expresses itself in the cosmic evolution and makes itself visible in this way. This means that all the atheists' attacks and criticisms thereby have no target. The giant enemy which atheism goes out to fight, namely, the extramundane image of the unfathomable ultimate reality which believers had constructed for themselves, changes into a windmill. Even Dawkins says that his criticism is only levelled at a supernatural

God, a *theos*. But because in normal pre-modern language the term "God" refers only to a *theos*, he wrongly thinks that he has to attack every religion.

But what exactly does Bonhoeffer mean by his statement about the world which has come of age, is more godless and therefore perhaps closer to God than the world which has not yet reached maturity? Before his two great letters he had often spoken of autonomy. In the two letters, instead of this expression he now uses the word responsible. By a responsible world he therefore means a world which has become aware of its autonomy. Such a world can only be atheistic because it has liberated itself from the notion of a *theos* which rules all and decides everything. The dependent world is therefore the world which is always pre-modern in its thinking and is characterized by the cult of a God who is outside the cosmos but who is only a transitional and inadequate reflection of the Ultimate Reality. In liberating itself from this view of things, the world gains richer access to this nameless transcendence which can be called the genuine God. A richer access, because theism also opens rich access to this transcendence. And not only monotheism opens it. Polytheism also does, although to a lesser extent. For every religion, even the most backward, is awakened by the fundamental reality of God in humanity to help man gradually to transcend the level of humanity which has already been achieved but which always remains inadequate. Religion is to free him of his self-centredness and thereby make him more capable of living as a fellow human being. And this means being compassionate.

This view does away with the contrast between the teaching of the church that we must receive our salvation from God and the conviction of modern humanism that man has to save himself. In fact these are two different ways of looking at a drawing of a cube. Depending on one's vantage point each person sees the same cube in a different form, one from above and one from below. For atheism, liberation cannot come from another world because there is no other world. It has to be born of the strong desire for humanization which is at work deep within us. But for the modern-thinking believer this desire is identical with the evolutionary drive within us, and this drive is the self-expression of Fundamental Love. Salvation therefore has nothing to do with a human sacrifice and the shedding of blood on the cross to persuade God to relent. Such language is pure mythology.

Translated into the language of modernity it means: Fundamental Love, God, is so intensely active in Jesus Christ that everyone who adheres to him through faith and follows him is granted a share of his great freedom. For salvation is only the church's parlance for becoming inwardly free and responsible, for liberation.

Cultural history shows that no culture acknowledges the full value of interpretations of God which are different from their own. Because of this, people again and again yielded to the temptation to impose their own religious ideas on others either by missionizing or by persecution. That is what monotheistic Christianity did to the world of the gods of antiquity, in the conviction that its own view was not only more valuable but was even the perfect and definitive one. And it held onto this conviction even when modernity gradually revealed the weaknesses of its image of God. These were, first of all, the extramundane character of the Christian *theos* for whom there is no longer any place in a secular culture; secondly, the related contradiction between a creator who determines all things and an autonomous cosmos; thirdly, the impossibility of reconciling the almighty power attributed to the *theos* with the infinite goodness likewise attributed to him, in other words: the thorny problem of evil and suffering; fourthly, the fact that he is superfluous with regard to explaining cosmic processes; and finally, the lack of any trace of his activity and his reality. Modernity had to conclude from all of this that such a *theos* – and this is the God of the three book-religions – no less than Baal or Jupiter, is the product of human imagination. It is a better thought out product and more auspicious, but it suffers from the same handicap: namely, that no reality corresponds to this image. Also this image of God is ultimately a human fabrication, made here and projected on high and burdened only too often with all-too-human ballast. The rock of modernity has started to move and is colliding now in the West against the earthen feet of this image of God – which is crumbling.

Faith which integrates atheism

What does a Christianity look like which corresponds to Bonhoeffer's intuition and is therefore not a foreign body in modern society? It has of necessity to integrate the theory of evolution. Without this integration no dialogue with modernity is possible. In the view of a modern Christianity the entire evolving cosmos, with man as its transitional high point, is the self-expression of an ultimate reality which, while conceptually unintelligible, can nevertheless be experienced. With our very inadequate concepts, however, we are able to say some things about this ultimate reality which are not devoid of meaning. First, that it must be dynamic, for its self-expression is characterized as evolution; second, that it has to be "life", since its self-expression is developed in the course of many billions of years from subatomic particles through the formation of atoms and then molecules and ever more complex protein compounds to living matter; further, that it must be "spirit", for this living material is developing infinitely slowly first into conscious matter and then into a form of consciousness of a superior kind: namely, the human spirit.

But if our spirit is a share in the infinite spirit itself, then not only is our own self deeply present behind every act of consciousness, but the Absolute Self is likewise present although at an even deeper level. This deeply implicit consciousness of the "Absolute", a consciousness which is present in all of us, is a transcendence experience. It is – much more than the inexplicability of natural phenomena and the fear associated with them – the foundation of the religious phenomenon and thus explains its omnipresence. Depending on the cultural phase in which societies functioned and were awakened by confrontation with either frightening or pleasant natural phenomena, this deeply implicit experience was converted into imaginable forms: Ra, Baal, Jupiter, Yahweh – all transitional forms. Because the fundamental reality is dynamic it cannot settle for what is only transitional. It reveals itself as a never-ending search for more adequate representations. That explains the development from poly- to monotheism and finally from mono- to a-theism. For even the one *theos* is a human design which does more justice to the ultimate reality than is the case with previous representations, but it is still not its adequate reflection.

Fundamental reality manifests itself, however, not only as life and consciousness and spirit but also as Fundamental Love. Evolution itself could lead the observer to suspect this. The self-expression of fundamental reality is characterized by the emergence of richer and richer linking forms, according to the law formulated by Teilhard de Chardin, of increasing complexity in increasing interiority until this search for connection becomes altruism (there are already clear promptings of this in the animal kingdom) and in man takes the form of selfless love. The experience of mystically gifted Jews then led to the conviction that Yahweh, in whom they tentatively found fundamental reality, was a loving God. And in the greatest son of the Jewish people, Jesus of Nazareth, this conviction deepened to become the conviction that God is love. He lived as a man for other human beings, breaking through normal levels of love for mankind in a way which he could not have learnt from his fellow men. His conviction must have welled up from a source deep within himself. Anyone who believed in a God who cared about human beings saw in him the effective presence of God, the reflection, the image of God. But this God of Israel is still only the *theos*, the God-in-Heaven and therefore only the finger that points to the ultimate, to the spiritual and loving depths which have no name. Through the way he appears, Jesus gives us, better than all other human manifestations, an idea of what these divine depths are like.

Turning to this Jesus of Nazareth, learning from him, following him, joins us more securely with the fundamental reality than does the Christian cult of God-in-Heaven, or the Church institution with its teaching and its liturgy. Anyone who wants to climb a mountain is well advised to watch the path in front of him over which he has to go step by step rather than always to be looking up at the peak. That means that in following the captivating humanity of Jesus we encounter ultimate reality more directly and in a richer way than in the cultic looking up to God-in-Heaven which is the concern of the institution Church.

In this whole representation of Christian thinking and acting there is nothing to which atheistic modernity could not subscribe, since in it the *theos* figure, the God-in-Heaven which has become untenable for modernity, has evaporated and disappeared. All that remains is the fundamental mystery, the essence of which is love.

Review and Epilogue

There is a deep rift between the thinking of the past and the thinking of modern man. The rift only opened up in the second half of the 18th century. While the church was building its spiritual as well as its secular city the split did not come about for a long time. When it finally arrived, it emerged that the church's city was on the wrong side of the divide – on the side of the past. The church still lived (both its leaders and the vast majority of its members) with the conviction that our tangible and always transitional world is completely dependent on a second, eternal world which, beyond our reach and outside our experience, intervenes in our world at will. This division into two worlds permeates the whole of church doctrine.

This church doctrine is a magnificent structure, the fruit of the ingenuity of the human mind. But once one has taken up residence on the other side of the divide, has built one's house there, affirms the autonomy of the cosmos and of man, one has the impression that that magnificent structure is only a castle in the air. We were speaking above about the drawing of a cube which can be seen as two different shapes, depending on whether it is viewed from above or from below, but it can never be seen in both shapes at the same time. It is normal to see only one shape and it is not an error to be unable to discover the other shape. But it is a bad mistake to maintain that there *is* no other and equally valid shape and to refuse all credibility to those who see another shape and describe it. This is precisely the error committed by pre-modern believers in condemning as heresy what is only another form of the same faith.

Modern believers, on the other hand, have no difficulty in accepting that the pre-modern view based on belief in an almighty, omniscient and to some extent anthropomorphic God-in-Heaven can be a correct expression of the Christian message. Furthermore, this expression can even be the original and therefore also an authentic expression of this message, for in the past no shape of the cube other than the pre-modern heteronomous one had been seen. And despite all the appalling things for which this church of the past can be blamed, it has still been a source of profound human enrichment. It has, in other words, had a rich "salutary" influence. Thinking heteronomously was not at all an error on its part, for it had to think that way, and so it is also today not an error that it still for the most part thinks that way, for the wheels of the mill of history turn slowly. But it is wrong when it stubbornly insists that the view of the cube with which it is familiar is the only possible one and therefore the only right one, and then condemns and persecutes those who see the cube differently and describe what follows from it for Christian thinking and living. In this way it makes its own message implausible for modern-thinking humanity. And what is its message for? Only for the good of mankind and therefore also for the good of modern-thinking humanity. If it adheres stubbornly to its views of old, the world of the future will be deprived of excellent opportunities for its healing, and the church itself will, in a world which, because of globalization, is more and more impregnated with modern views, fade away to become a marginal phenomenon taken less and less seriously.

The modern believer realizes the validity and coherence of the traditional formulation of the Christian message as it is presented at length in the *Catechism of the Catholic Church*. But he can no longer accept as useful the foundation of this construction: the belief in an almighty omniscient *theos*. Like modern atheism he says that this God-in-Heaven does not exist. In the eyes of the faithful who have remained pre-modern, such unbelief is clearly a capitulation to the spirit of the age with which modern believers (who are deemed no longer worthy of the name) have become too friendly. Anyone who sleeps with the dog wakes up with fleas. Fortunately, pre-modern believers probably will not open this book. Otherwise they would see in Chapter Seven that the belief which is in keeping with our time, taken to its logical conclusion, has to end in a rejection of a *theos*, a God-in-Heaven, and therefore in a-theism. This would be for them the clearest proof that the thinking of modernity is the work of the "father of lies" (John 8:44), alias the devil.

One can level two criticisms against their honest worry about orthodoxy. The first is that it rejects *a priori* the possibility of a second equally valid form of doctrine. This is the way the cardinals reacted when Galileo invited them to look through the telescope and to observe Jupiter's moons with their own eyes. Because the moons did not exist, wanting to see them made no sense. And acting nonsensically is ethically wrong. But modern man sees the other form of faith only too clearly, and to deny its possibility excludes modern humanity – basically future humanity – from the joyous message. It is a great disaster for them, but also, as we have said, a great disaster for the church which the pre-modern faithful deeply love and for which they want only the best.

The second criticism is that it deserves the reproach which the prophet Elijah in 1 Kings 18:20 levels at a gathering of the Israelites: that it is wavering between two opinions. Well into the 19th century, for example, the pre-modern church leadership vigorously condemned democracy. It could not be otherwise: in its system of thinking, all power comes from God-in-Heaven and not, as in the constitution of modern states, from the people. But in the 20th century it gradually (and rightly) changed direction and became the advocate of this democracy which it had earlier sharply condemned and which it now considered the best form of government, at least outside its own theocratic dominion. One can label that as opportunism and accuse the church leadership, and not without cause, of telling modernity what it wants to hear. Opportunism or not, it is certainly a wavering between two opinions. It is not possible to affirm human autonomy and at the same time deny it. And the democratic idea is the fruit of modernity's way of thinking. Anyone who praises it affirms at least implicitly the autonomy of man and of society. And affirms therefore the thinking of the Enlightenment.

This example (one of many) is asking the question: does the church leadership accept the autonomy of man and of the cosmos and therefore the basic ideas of enlightened modernity or does it not accept them? Surely it cannot secretly keep on shifting from one to the other just to avoid embarrassment in today's world? But unfortunately that is exactly what the church constantly does, without realizing it. It shifts from a pre-modern way of observing the cube to the other way, depending on circumstances. Does the grass on the other side of the divide which opened up with the Enlightenment look much greener? Then why does the church not decide to go there to live? Because an exodus is always a painful undertaking. The church is consistent in praising the obedience of Abraham when he received the summons: "Leave your homeland, your people, and your father's family and go into a foreign land that I will show you." It would do well to copy this obedience of the father of its faith. Meantime, with the warming of the modern spiritual climate the ecclesiastical iceberg is inexorably melting away under the waterline. The day is coming when it will go down with great commotion.

What will happen when this exodus occurs? In this book and in the previous one, *Living in God without God*, some important steps are described in detail. The first is the transition from traditional law-based ethics to an ethics based on love. This was dealt with in *Living in God without God*. Everything that used to be commanded or forbidden on the authority of God-in-Heaven loses its binding force. Our further human development, as the modern believer sees it, is exclusively the fruit of the growth of love in us. Hence an act is good or bad according to the amount of love – or lack of it – which is incorporated in it. The consequences are explained there in detail.

But to live in God without the God of the monotheistic tradition includes more than just the new ethic which was the limited scope of the previous book. It must also have consequences for prayer, since prayer is essentially encounter with "God" and will itself have to change with the change in our conception of God. Both personal prayer and liturgical prayer will take on a different hue. That is the second step, and it was dealt with in Chapter Two of this book.

The transition from the pre-modern faith to a faith which is in tune with modernity also leads to a different attitude to the Bible. That is the third step, which is dealt with in Chapters Three and Four. The modern believer, namely, can no longer read the Bible as one used to read it and as the church leadership still reads it today: as a book with the infallible words of God-in-Heaven. For the modern believer they are human words, witness to the divine experiences of those people to whom we owe the beginning of the tradition of our faith. They expressed their experiences of the divine in conceptual categories which had their origin in a different cultural world. At this point Bible criticism arrived on the scene and tried to sift the gold out of the sand: the permanence of the divine experience was sifted from the time-conditioned culture of the authors. And again the church leaders look in both directions at once. After decades of expressly condemning it they at last approve of Bible criticism and accept that it is permitted to dissect Bible texts as human documents. But here it is in glaring contradiction with its proclaimed unity of divine and human authorship, which is not explained in detail, and with its requirement to conclude the Bible reading at Mass with the exclamation "Word of the living God". But when the author is God himself (he is seen to remain as author even though with human collaboration) his sacred words surely cannot be laid on the dissecting table! Modern believers, on the other hand, only acknowledge a human author. But when this author expresses his divine experiences they know that the divine mystery he has encountered is present in the core of what he writes. Unfortunately, because of the deep cultural divide between biblical authors and modern readers or listeners the divine message does not get through the human utterances. Then there is nothing left of the word of God, and the Bible text is then simply human words. The Bible is like a gold mine: many tons of stone and a few ounces of gold.

But the whole of Christian doctrine is built on the words of the Bible. Contact with this tradition is indispensable, and here great danger is threatening. The Bible is human language. It is based, on the one hand, on the wordless speaking of God in the depths of inspired persons who have tried to give expression to it in human words, and on the other hand, it is based on his wordless speaking in us which lets us hear his speech although it is poured out in human words. For God's eternal wordless speech to be able to reach us through those time-conditioned human words it must necessarily be peeled out of the husk of its inadequate formulations. And that is what Bible criticism attempts to do. It is to protect us from divinizing human words, from taking time-related words for eternal words. That is the reason for the critical treatment of the Bible in Chapters Three and Four. This was also necessary for the reason that the weight of tradition is so heavy that it drags down even modern-thinking believers into the quicksand of pre-modern thought. Only an alert mind can preserve itself from this danger.

The turning from the heteronomous to the modern conception of God means a small revolution also in the way we handle the liturgy. Chapters Five and Six dealt with this in detail. They were limited to consideration of the Eucharist, but in any case the average believer has little contact with other liturgical forms, and what was said in these two chapters about the liturgy of the Mass applies also to the rest of the liturgy.

As such, the liturgy is the ritual way in which we give shape to our shared encounter with God as Christians. Church authorities like to describe the liturgy as "sacred", perhaps in order to tell the people to keep its hands off and, instead, to follow exactly what is prescribed by the authorities – in this case, the Vatican's Liturgy Commission. In the eyes of this commission the liturgy is a totality of untouchable rituals which come from on high and which the commission accepts and requires the rest of the faithful to accept. "Sacred" is meant to convey that those rituals have to do with the almighty second world which insists that, for those appearing before the divine ruler, the ceremonial procedures prescribed by him have to be exactly observed. But "sacred" means in reality that someone or something is a small self-expression of Fundamental Love and is therefore healing and beneficial. A sublime ritual, as for example a Papal Mass in St Peter's Cathedral, can definitely be attractive and psychologically beneficial. But that is something different from remembrance, in common faith, of the actions of Jesus at the Last Supper where he symbolically gives himself to his fellow men. And exact observance of prescriptions from the early Middle Ages hardly has anything to do with this remembrance. These prescriptions were made a thousand years ago by people belonging to a culture that has since died out and they reflect the spirit of that culture. Of course they corresponded to the needs of their time. But a community which is modern in its faith often hardly knows what to do with these texts and can no longer take the prescriptions seriously. What used to be good and suited to the age does not remain eternally good and certainly not suited to the age for very long. We should therefore search for a modern inner-worldly form to use for our common encounter with the divine depths. With the richness of tradition to guide us we should create for modern people a liturgy which is appropriate to the time. That is the fourth step. That this is forbidden by church authorities has nothing to do with it. We should obey God more than men.

One remark in conclusion. The church authorities were criticized above for sometimes giving up their heteronomous position in favour of the autonomy of believers, an autonomy which they otherwise condemn, so that they waver between the two sides. The same danger, but in reverse, threatens modern believers: namely, that they fall back on the procedures and behaviour of the pre-modern past. This past has been hammered into us. We are unable to cast it off like an old garment. Instead, it sticks to our skin. That is why we are far from drawing all the conclusions involved in a modern believer's point of view.

This book has tried to show some of these conclusions which can easily be overlooked. The words "freedom of the children of God" have not been mentioned. However, everything has been aimed at clearing the path to this precious freedom from all hindrances and stumbling blocks. It is up to the reader to judge whether this attempt has been helpful.